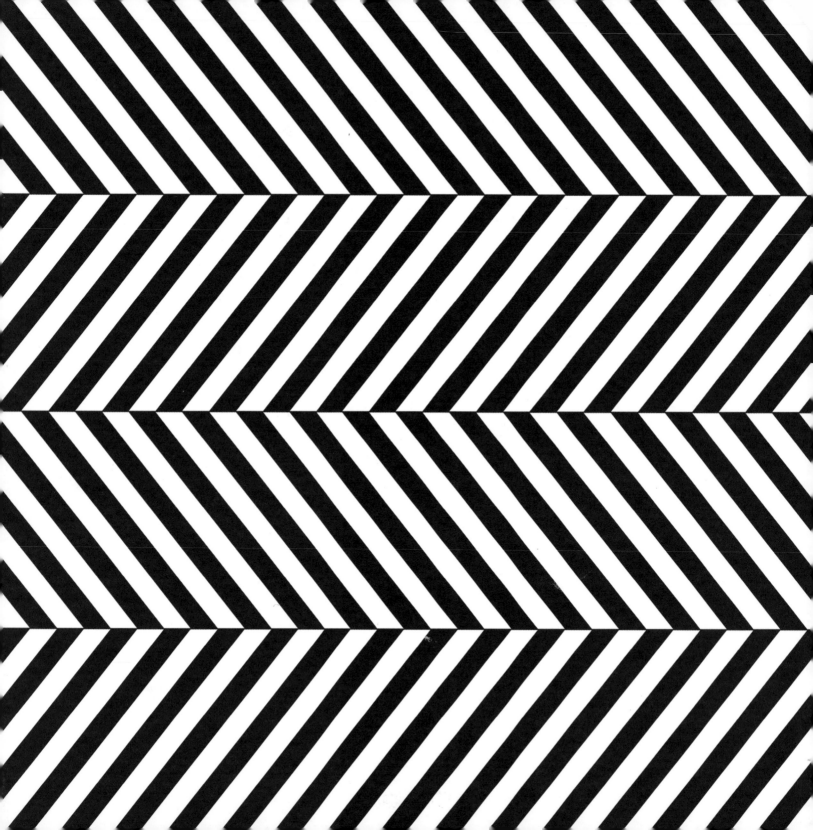

JUST
SEW
STORIES

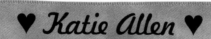

♥ Katie Allen ♥

25 SPECTACULAR CRAFTY GIFTS TO SEW

hardie grant books
MELBOURNE · LONDON

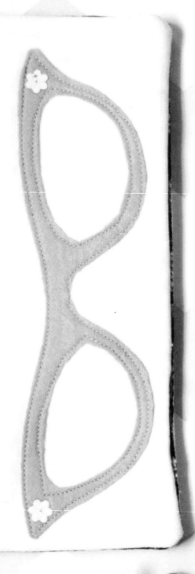

PROP AGAN DA

Membership 2011

theWI INSPIRING WOMEN

Ruth Bond

CONTENTS

'I COULD MAKE THAT'

Any time I go shopping with my mother or my nan, it won't be long before one of us says the famous four words, 'I could make that'. Whether we actually can, or ever do, doesn't matter – we've just all got the itch to stitch.

I come from a family of DIY-ers. My mum can whip up a pair of curtains in a day and, when we were younger, my brother and I were frequently dressed in her appliquéd and smocked '80s creations (more fun for me than him, I should think). My Nanny Rita is an expert knitter and her late husband, my Grandad Bill, built me dolls' houses as well as a boat that the whole family holidayed in. My father's side of the family has artists and gardeners galore, and give him some fibreglass and some kind of ratchet and he'll build you a car.

It was no wonder then that I grew up loving to make things – clay food and miniature clothes for my dolls' houses, jewellery that you bake in the oven, papier maché bowls, glittery projects from *Just Seventeen* magazine. As I grew older I customised charity shop bargains and hand-painted slogans on T-shirts. A skate punk who couldn't skate, I added swathes of denim to make my jeans even wider, stitched patches to rucksacks and threaded hundreds of bead bracelets.

Along the way I've fallen for beading, knitting, cross-stitch, embroidery and dress-making – and still little excites me more than rummaging through remnants bins or spools of ribbon and making things out of them. It's even more exciting now you can go online and buy Japanese Kokka fabric or buttons off Etsy and read craft blogs from somewhere in Glasgow or Minnesota or Sydney.

Craft is international now. It's big. Once the preserve of apparent weirdos such as myself who collected lollipop sticks and bits of foil that 'could be useful' – it's cool, it's sociable. People host craft and cocktail nights – there are classes in lampshade-making and lino-cutting.

Many people have credited Debbie Stoller, editor of US feminist magazine *Bust* and founder of the Stitch 'n Bitch movement – which made it cool for young knitters to bring their yarn and their yakking to cafés and bars – for kick-starting the craft revolution. And I know she, and *Bust*, had a massive impact on me – particularly for celebrating the feminist aspect of crafting. Of course loads of boys craft (I remember my Grandad Derek telling me about the socks chaps knitted during the war) but sewing and knitting and the like were looked down on until recently, because they were things women did – in the home, quietly, while the men did the important stuff. And later some women themselves rejected crafting as a symbol of domestic oppression.

Today, crafters are turning that idea on its head and simply celebrating the joy of making things and learning how to do it together. You can jar jam or knit blankets or embroider handkerchiefs or felt eensy deer to perch just-so in a terrarium – and you can do it beautifully and professionally or just for fun; you can do it for profit; you can do it for charity; you can do it for environmental reasons; you can do it to subvert the system (such as the protest movement Craftivism); you can do it to feed and clothe yourself and your family; you can do it as a frivolous indulgence in fine silk and colourful braid; you can do it to feel creative and get your hands dirty; or you can do it just as an excuse to turn the damn computer off/put the smartphone down.

And, yeah, it may seem selfish to squander quids we don't have on those cute vintage buttons, or to hide our fabric stash under the pillows, but crafters have the last laugh in that we can always make something for someone else – and homemade presents always go down a storm.

There's nothing nicer than giving (or, yes, receiving) a truly awesome gift because everything you make for yourself, or for someone else, is a story in itself – the colours you pick, the fabrics you choose, the time you spend, and how you wrap it up and give it to them . . . which is why I wrote the book you are holding right now.

I hope you enjoy my *Just Sew Stories*, and that you also feel 'I could make that'.

Katie x

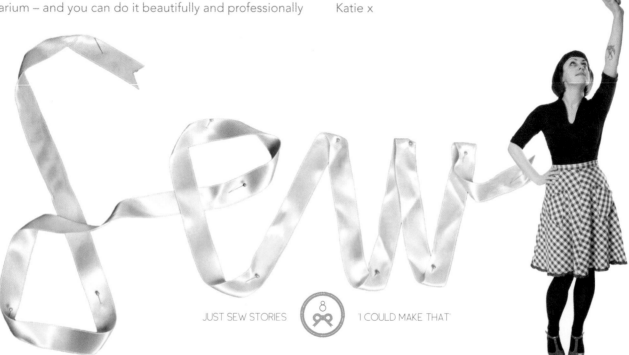

BEFORE YOU GET STARTED

DON'T FORGET

To have a successful crafting day you need to batten down the hatches and focus. These five things will help you along the way.

1. Food: Cake is not food. Well it is, but if you are planning to indulge in a hardcore crafting weekend then you will need sustenance of the vegetables and protein kind too.

2. A kettle (or reliable friend who can swing by with coffee): Tea/hot beverages have been proven essential to the crafting process

3. Good lighting: Squinting at needles adds ten years to your face you know.

4. A table: Basically, something flat to cut on and spread out your wares. A floor will do, depending on your knees.

5. Pin cushion/a magnet: You *will* get pins in the carpet/rug/your foot.

THE BASICS

Every serious crafter needs to have the following in their kit before getting started:

SCISSORS
Get some decent fabric scissors – Fiskars is a good brand. Don't use them to cut paper as it will blunt the blades.

FABRIC PEN/TAILOR'S CHALK
You can buy different sorts of fabric pens. I prefer to use water-soluble pens which can be dabbed away with a bit of damp cotton wool. Tailor's chalk or pencils are also very handy.

TAPE MEASURE
To measure things. A clear plastic ruler/set square is also very useful, especially for patchwork.

SEAM RIPPER
These little tools are super handy for ripping out wrong stitches – and are much quicker than using nail scissors, let me tell you!

SEWING MACHINE
Janome, Brother, Bernina and Singer are all good brands – the more stitch options the machine has the pricier it will be, but you really only need a few to make almost anything. You should get a range of needles (generally the finer the fabric, the finer the needle you should use) and sewing feet with the machine – otherwise a zip foot will be a handy purchase. And don't forget a packet of bobbins (the small plastic spools which carry the bottom thread on your machine).

The smaller the stitches you use, the tougher the sewing. A zigzag stitch is good for stretch fabric – but keep an eye on the stitch width as the needle will be moving from side to side rather than forwards. Test on a scrap before you start sewing.

NEEDLES
A pack of multi-sized needles will do you fine. As before, in general, the finer the fabric the thinner the needle you will need.

Needles for everyday use have very small, round eyes and are known as sharps. Embroidery or crewel needles have a larger, longer eye for thicker threads. Needles for cross-stitching have a larger eye and a blunt tip. You may also need yarn needles for stitching yarn – these are made of plastic or metal and are quite thick and blunt. Beading needles are also good for fine work with beads or sequins – these are very long and thin.

Pins are also necessary – ball-head pins are colourful and easy to use (and easy to spot if you drop them).

SEWING THREAD
Polycotton is best for everyday use and works with both hand and machine sewing. Cotton thread has little give to it, so is not as suitable for stretchy fabric – try polyester thread instead. Gutermann and Coats are good brands.

AN IRON AND IRONING BOARD
To get rid of any pesky creases in your fabric.

INTERFACING
This can be sew-in or fusible – I prefer the latter as you can just steam it in place with a hot iron. It helps support and firm-up fabric. Fusible web can be used to join pieces of fabric together without sewing.

FABRIC

Most of the projects in this book use cotton or polycotton. Cotton is natural and non-stretchy, while polyester is tough and creases less. A mix of the two is good for most crafty projects.

Cotton twill or canvas materials are good for projects that need to be durable, such as tote bags – you could also use denim, but don't forget to change the needle on your machine to a denim needle.

Some fabrics have a 'right' and a 'wrong' side – the right side is the one you want to be seen.

Wash and press your chosen fabric before you use it – as it can shrink if you wash your projects later.

Felt is an absolute dream for craft projects as it is tough and doesn't fray. The thicker the felt, the better the quality.

USEFUL EXTRAS

* Craft knife and mat
* Embroidery hoop
* Fabric glue
* Paint brushes
* Pencils/crayons/felt tips
* Pinking shears (scissors with zigzag teeth which help prevent fabric fraying)
* Poppers/press studs
* Pritt Stick/Copydex or similar glues
* PVA glue or Modge Podge
* Safety pins
* Stuffing wadding (known as batting in the US) – polyester wadding is fine for small projects, while cotton wadding is better for quilts
* Washi tape (Japanese masking tape)
* Plus always keep an eye out for zips, buttons, glitter, sequins, beads, yarn, ribbon, lace and bias binding

CRAFTACULAR PLAYLIST

'Lawdy Miss Clawdy' – Lloyd Price
'Mystery Train Kept A Rollin'' – Stray Cats
'Horses' – Patti Smith (to be played over and over again)
'Rumours' – Fleetwood Mac (ditto)
'Human Fly' – The Cramps
'Train in Vain' – The Clash
'Shake It' – David Bowie
'Daniel' – Bat for Lashes
'Shaking Paper' – Cat Power
'Sophia' – Laura Marling

STITCH GUIDE

BACK STITCH

Back stitch is a tough but neat way of stitching straight lines.

Bring your needle up through the fabric and make a small stitch, going in the opposite direction to the way you want your line of stitching to go. Then bring the needle back up a stitch-length ahead of where you began sewing. Push it back through in your original hole. Bring it up again a stitch-length ahead. Repeat.

SATIN STITCH

Satin stitch is an easy way to fill large spaces. Make a large stitch across the space you have to fill. Loop the needle round underneath and come back up just next to your original hole. Make another stitch, making sure your thread lies snugly next to the first stitch. Repeat.

CHAIN STITCH

Chain stitch is a little tricky to get started but once you get going it's a beaut.

Knot the end of your embroidery thread and bring the needle up through the fabric where you want your stitch to begin. Pull the thread taut, then push your needle back down through the hole you've just made. As the thread runs through, catch the last little bit in a loop and hold it under your thumb.

Now poke your needle up through the fabric where you want your next stitch to start, and hook it through the loop you have just made. Gently pull it tight, and start again, putting your needle into the previous loop.

WHIP STITCH

Whip stitch is a neat way to join two folded edges of fabric.

Thread your needle and knot the end of the cotton thread. Holding the two horizontal folded edges before you, push the needle through the nearest edge, from wrong side to right side, as close to the edge as you can. This will hide the knot inside your seam.

Pull through until the knot catches, then bring your needle round to the back of the two pieces, and push through both pieces of fabric, making a tiny stitch. Keep going along the two edges, moving in a loop from back to front and to the back again. Fasten off with a few stitches in place. Pull the loop taut and continue.

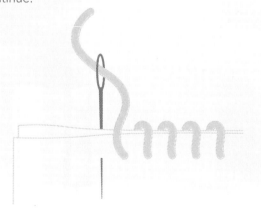

BLANKET STITCH

Blanket stitch is a nice decorative edging and also helps stop fraying.

Knot the end of your embroidery thread and bring the needle up through the fabric a short distance from the edge. Pull through until the knot catches. Staying on the front of the fabric, insert your needle about 1 cm (⅜ inch) along the fabric at the same level as the start of the first stitch.

Pull the needle through from back to front, catching the loop you have made. As you pull the thread it should form the shape of the blanket stitch along the edge of the fabric. To continue, make another stitch about 1 cm (⅜ inch) along from the first stitch.

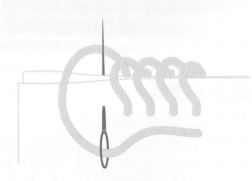

STEM STITCH

Stem stitch is a nice smooth stitch which is useful for marking out lines in embroidery.

Bring your thread up through the fabric and make a smallish stitch, angling very slightly to the right. Bring the needle up again to the left of your original stitch, and about half-way along. Make another stitch, again slightly angled to the right. Keep the stitches snuggled tight for a smooth line. Keep going.

As you get practised, you will be able to push the needle through the fabric and back up in position for the next stitch in one movement, which is much neater.

STRAIGHT STITCH

Straight stitch pretty much does what it says on the tin. Large straight stitches are known as tacking and can be used to temporarily join fabric.

Thread your needle and knot the end of the cotton thread, then simply weave the needle in and out of the fabric in a straight line. Easy!

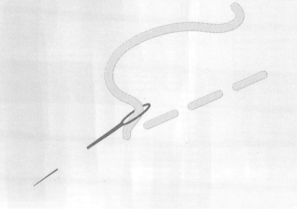

1.
easy as pie

BLOW ON IT

Handkerchiefs have a bad rep as a lazy present for grandparents – but, as ever, the older generation have it licked, style-wise. An embroidered handkerchief is far classier than a manky wedge of tissues – and looks smarter folded into the top pocket of your boy's suit.

My secret messages add a touch of snark – add them to a hanky for your woeful pal and distract them from their latest break-up/broken nail/repeat viewing of *Sleepless in Seattle*.

MATERIALS

* Embroidery thread
* Lace/rick-rack braid
* Matching sewing thread
* White cotton, 30 cm x 30cm (12 inches x 12 inches) for each handkerchief

EQUIPMENT

* Cotton wool
* Embroidery hoop
* Embroidery needle
* Iron and ironing board
* Paper
* Pins
* Sewing machine or sewing needle
* Water soluble fabric marker pen

MAKE THE HANDKERCHIEF

1. Press your square of fabric.

2. Fold over the tiniest hem along one edge, press, and then fold over on itself again. If you are sewing by hand, use whip stitch (see p. 14) to close, or use a small straight stitch on your sewing machine. Hem all four sides and press again.

3. If you are going for a plain, masculine look, leave your handkerchief blank but I always say if there is an excuse for embellishment, go for it! Pink lace will add a lady-like look, white rick-rack braid is a more old-fashioned and subtle decoration, while black lace gives that Victorian-in-mourning gothic vibe.

4. Pin the lace in place on the right side of the hanky. It is easier to hand stitch lace. Use white sewing thread, which will look less messy on the reverse of your handkerchief, but try to use tiny stitches.

5. Sew the lace to all four sides of your hanky. Press.

ADD THE EMBROIDERY

1. First, decide on your message – the fewer words the better. Use a corner of your paper and write it out as clearly as you can on a diagonal to the two straight edges of the paper.

   A larger version of your handwriting adds a personal touch or copy a stylised free font off the internet. Go over your message again – it needs to be bold.

2. Place the corner of your handkerchief over your paper, matching up the edges. Trace the message using the fabric pen.

3. Choose a colour of embroidery thread and pull out two strands. Thread through your embroidery needle and knot the end. Follow the lines of your message in stem stitch (see p. 15) and finish off with a couple of neat stitches in place. Dab away the pen marks with damp cotton wool.

4. Press your handkerchief. To make it an extra special present, roll up neatly and tie with a matching ribbon.

ALTERNATIVELY . . .

Make four handkerchiefs out of brightly coloured cotton – and *voila*, you have napkins. Embroider gastronomic messages such as 'Eat up!'; 'Nom nom nom'; 'Elbows off the table'; 'Pass the salt!' on the corners.

Boo
hoo...

LETTERS OF LOVE

There's nothing sadder than a bare wall, especially when you're too old for Green Day posters (ahem) and can't afford proper art. Solution? Make something!

These beframed beauties are super quick to stitch and sling on the vertical. Spell out your boyfriend/girlfriend's name, the initials of your betrothed or your friends, or go gothic and try 'love' and 'hate' for new housemates.

Because I haven't used traditional aida (cross-stitch fabric) but plain cotton, it would be easy enough to swap for something more overstated – try flowery fabric with gold-stitched letters, or red stitches on blue and white stripes for a nautical effect.

MATERIALS

* Embroidery thread
* White cotton fabric (cut a piece about 10 cm (4 inches) larger all the way around than your frame)

EQUIPMENT

* Cotton wool
* Embroidery hoop
* Embroidery needle
* Iron and ironing board
* Scissors
* Water soluble fabric marker pen

FRAMING

I used rubber wood-effect embroidery hoops that doubled up as vintage-looking frames for my letters. If you can't find these, do your stitching in ordinary embroidery hoops and then transfer the fabric to your chosen picture frame. If it's an open frame, you will have to stretch the fabric taut and pin in place with tacks or staples on the back of the frame. If your frame is glazed, take off the back and stretch out the fabric – use picture-framing tape to hold down the edges. Then put the back of the frame in place again; you may need to tape this down too.

Or you could just leave your fabric in the embroidery hoop for a simple, crafty look.

TO MAKE

1. Press your fabric. Loosen your embroidery hoop and separate the two circles. Place your fabric over the inner hoop and wedge the other one back over the top. You may have to tighten it up again.

2. Using the fabric pen, mark out your chosen letter with a dot for the start and end of each stitch. I just made up my own letter style, but if you need some guidance follow the pattern opposite.

3. Thread your needle with two strands of embroidery thread and knot the end. Now you're ready to sew!

   Always try to sew your cross-stitches the same way, e.g. moving from bottom left to top right all along a row, then go back to complete the stitches, moving from bottom right to top left. This means the light will shine off the letters the same way and it will look much prettier.

   Try to keep it as neat as you can on the back – finish off by weaving the thread back through a couple of stitches. Trim any loose ends.

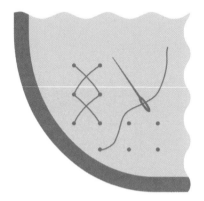

4. Once you've finished your letter, use damp cotton wool to blot out the pen marks.

5. Turn the finished piece over and trim the fabric close to the inner hoop. And you're done!

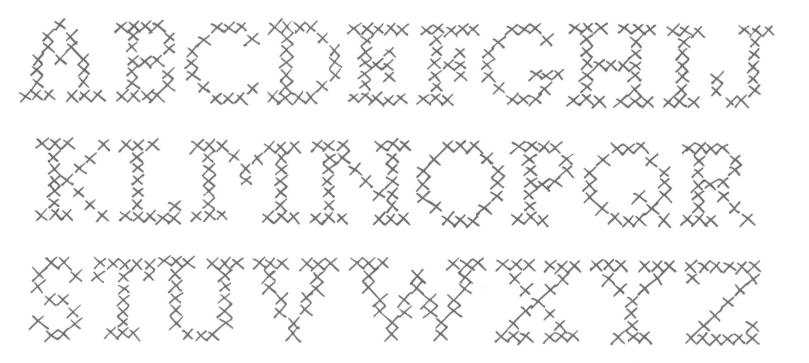

A B C D E F G H I J

K L M N O P Q R

S T U V W X Y Z

LIVEN UP YOUR WALL

I think lots of pictures and embroideries in mismatched frames bring a wall to life. One of my favourite cafes is Cake Hole in East London – a little nook behind the vintage crockery and linen ware shop Vintage Heaven on Columbia Road. Its walls are jam-packed with retro embroideries, paintings and photographs as cluttered and crazy as the

Find frames at car-boot and jumble sales and in charity shops. If that so-awesome frame comes with a not-so-awesome painting or embroidery inside, it's easy enough to whip out the offending article and, if you have the same kitsch taste as me, recycle it on a birthday card, decoupage it with some PVA glue on an old tray – or use the

CHECKMATE

I love, love, love a dapper chap in a bow tie (I'm talking daywear, with smart braces and something tweedy – no purple satin here) and I think, secretly, boys like wearing them too.

Make your beau a bow tie from some pre-loved fabric (I used scraps from a charity shop shirt) for extra softness. If he's really into co-ordinating, run up a matching pocket square (see the handkerchief pattern on p. 19) or use leftover fabric to line a glasses case (see p. 53) for full matchy-matchy mathlete allure.

MATERIALS

- Bow tie clasp
- Checked cotton, 20 cm x 50 cm (8 inches x 19¾ inches)
- Iron-on interfacing, 30 cm x 20 cm (12 inches x 8 inches)
- Matching sewing thread
- Wide white elastic, 1 cm (⅜ inch)

EQUIPMENT

- Cotton wool
- Iron and ironing board
- Pins
- Scissors
- Sewing machine or sewing needle
- Water soluble fabric marker pen

HOW TO MAKE THE BOW

1. If your fabric is a charity shop bargain, it's probably best to give it a quick wash before using – otherwise you'll never get rid of that strange mothball smell.

2. Once it's dry, give it a good press. Make a pattern using the template below. Fold some white paper or tracing paper in half. With the fold at the dotted line, draw around the template. Cut out, unfold and pin to your fabric. Cut around the pattern then remove the pins. Repeat so you have two pieces.

3. Cut a rectangle of the interfacing that's a little larger than your pattern.

4. Following the manufacturer's instructions, press the interfacing onto the wrong side of one of your bow tie pieces. Whatever you do, make sure you get the interfacing around the right way (sticky side down) – otherwise you will ruin your iron!

5. Trim the interfacing to the same shape as your fabric.

6. Place your two bow tie pieces right sides together and pin. Stitch all the way around the bow tie shape, leaving a 5 mm (¼ inch) seam allowance. Leave a small gap.

7. Trim the corners off, being careful not to cut the stitches, and snip along the curved edges.

8. Turn the bow tie shape right sides out through the gap you left. Poke out the shape using a chopstick or pencil, then press flat, tucking in the raw edges of the gap.

9. Whip stitch (see p. 14) the gap closed and press again.

10. Now fold the two short ends of your piece in together – things should start looking more like a bow tie now! Use tiny whip stitches to sew them neatly together.

11. Arrange the loop you have made so the seam is at the back. Thread your needle and make a line of running stitches along that seam through both sides of the bow tie. Pull gently to gather the bow tie into a nice plump shape. Stitch in place to hold.

TEMPLATE: ACTUAL SIZE

MAKE THE NECK STRAP

1. Your bow tie strap will need to be about 5 cm (2 inches) shorter than the circumference of your beloved's neck, and 6 cm (2⅜ inches) wide. Cut a piece of these dimensions from your checked fabric. Fold in the short ends and press flat.

2. Fold the rectangle in half lengthways and press. Open up and fold each long edge into this centre fold and press. Fold in half again down the centre fold, and press. Pin in place.

3. Cut two 6 cm (2⅜ inch) pieces of the elastic. Thread one through half of your bow tie clasp and tuck the ends inside one end of your bow tie strap, leaving about 1.5 cm (⅝ inch) of elastic showing. Pin. Thread the other piece through the other half of the bow tie clasp and tuck the ends into the other end of your bow tie strap. Pin. Make sure the clasp halves are the right way round so they will link up properly.

4. Now sew across the short end of your bow tie strap (through the elastic), down the open side of the strap, and across the other short end.

PUT IT ALL TOGETHER

Now it's time to put things all together.

1. Cut a 10 cm x 6 cm (4 inch x 2⅜ inch) rectangle from your checked fabric. Fold each short side a tiny way onto the wrong side and press flat. Fold in half lengthways and press. Open out, and fold each long edge into the centre fold and press. The raw edges will now all be hidden.

2. Place your bow tie onto the centre point of your neck strap (fold it in half and mark with the fabric pen to make sure you have the central point). Stitch it in place.

3. Now take the little strip you have just made, and wind it round the centre of your bow tie (neat side facing out), including the neck strap, folding one end over the other on the back. It should be really snug. Use whip stitch to sew the end of the little strap in place.

4. And you're done!
   Très smart.

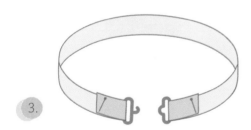

WRAP IT UP SCARF

Every year I promise to knit someone a scarf for Christmas and every year I never quite get round to it. If you find yourself in the same situation, ditch the needles and make this fleecy scarf instead. It's ridiculously quick to knock together, especially as fleece doesn't fray, so only the absolute minimum of pesky hemming is required.

This scarf is also mega long, perfect for looping round several times, and – extra bonus – it also doubles up as gloves so the lucky recipient can keep their neck and their mitts toasty warm at the same time. Two presents in one!

MATERIALS

* Fleece fabric, 20 cm x 320 cm (8 inches x 126 inches)
* Matching sewing thread

EQUIPMENT

* Cotton wool
* Iron and ironing board
* Pins
* Scissors
* Sewing machine or sewing needle
* Water soluble fabric marker pen

BEFORE YOU START

1. Take a good look at your fleece rectangle: one side will be fluffier than the other. Decide which one you prefer – this is the 'right side' and will be the most prominent.

2. You may need to join two 20 cm (8 inch) wide strips of fleece together to make a long enough piece for your scarf. To join, place the right sides together and sew along one short side, 1 cm (⅜ inch) from the edge.

   Open the fabric and lay it flat, right side down, so that the two raw edges are sticking up. Fold them flat against the wrong side of the fabric, one on top of the other, and pin. Stitch down, as close to the edges as you can. Remove pins and press.

MAKING THE POCKETS

1. Take one end of the scarf and lay it wrong side up. Fold the raw edge over 1 cm (⅜ inch), then over again another 1 cm (⅜ inch). Press flat and stitch along, as close to the edge as you can. Press again.

1.

2. Turn the piece over, right side up.

3. To make your design, mark out a line 18 cm (7 inches) from the end of your scarf with pins. Keeping within the square you have made, sketch out a shape with your fabric pen. I went for a wee heart, but any shape looks good – just keep it simple. Remember to do it 'upside down' from the end of your scarf – you're going to fold this piece back on itself to make the pocket. Take out the pins.

4. Sew your shape with the sewing machine – I used matching thread but a contrasting colour would look good too. Don't fasten off the ends. Instead thread the extra lengths onto a needle and take them through to the wrong side of the fabric. Fasten off as neatly as you can on the wrong side.

5. Fold the end of the scarf over, wrong sides together, until your pocket measures 18 cm (17 inches) high. Pin in place and stitch each side closed – start at the top (the open end of the pocket) as close to the edge as you can and whizz to the bottom. Leaving the needle down in the fabric, raise the machine foot and turn the scarf by 180 degrees. Put the foot down and whizz back up to give a doubly-strong seam.

WRONG SIDE

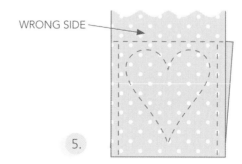

5.

6. When you reach the top again, leave the needle down, lift the foot, and turn the scarf 45 degrees. Put the foot down again and add a diagonal row of stitches about 5 cm (2 inches) long. This will stop your pockets gaping.

7. Press. Now do the other end of your scarf.

TIME FOR TEA

Who doesn't love a brew? These sweet reusable teabags are quick and easy to make for the tea fan in your life.

Mix and match the beads to co-ordinate with their favourite blends (red for raspberry, purple for fruit, green for, er, green). If you're feeling really generous, give the teabags with a matching teacup and saucer – and a box of loose tea, too, of course!

MATERIALS

- ❊ 1 flower bead
- ❊ 2 small wooden beads
- ❊ Clear nail varnish (if required)
- ❊ Fine but strong cotton thread
- ❊ Loose tea leaves (do not break open a teabag!)
- ❊ Matching sewing thread
- ❊ Unbleached linen or open weave cotton 18 cm x 10.5 cm (7$\frac{1}{16}$ inches x 4$\frac{1}{8}$ inches)

EQUIPMENT

- ❊ Embroidery needle with large eye
- ❊ Iron and ironing board
- ❊ Pins
- ❊ Scissors
- ❊ Sewing machine or sewing needle

MAKE THE BAG

1. Your fabric is unlikely to have a 'right' or 'wrong' side so simply lie it in front of you horizontally. Firstly, make the channel for your cotton thread. Turn the top long edge of your rectangle over 5 mm (¼ inch) and press flat. Then turn over another 1 cm (⅜ inch) and press flat. Pin in place.

2. Using a straight stitch (see p. 15), by hand or on the machine, sew along the bottom edge of your fold, keeping as close to the bottom of the fold as you can. Take out the pins and press again.

3. Turn your rectangle over, so the channel is on the underneath.

4. Cut about 30 cm (12 inches) of the cotton thread and thread your embroidery needle. Use the needle to punch a hole in the top side of the channel you have made, about 2 cm (¾ inch) in from the edge. Push the needle along the channel, being careful not to snag it, and poke it back out around 2 cm (¾ inch) from the other side. Pull your thread through, to leave equal lengths each side.

5. Fold the rectangle in half, so the channel side is on the outside. Keep the drawstrings tucked inside. Pin.

6. Sew, using a small back stitch if you are sewing by hand (see p. 13) or a zigzag with short stitch-lengths on your machine, down the open side of your bag and along the bottom, leaving a 1 cm (⅜ inch) hem. Be careful not to catch your drawstrings.

7. Trim any excess fabric, then turn the bag the right way out. Press flat.

8. Thread a wooden bead onto one drawstring and knot the end of your thread to stop the bead falling off. You may need a touch of clear nail varnish to seal it.

9. Thread a flower bead and a wooden bead onto the other drawstring, knot the thread and add nail varnish if necessary.

10. Add a spoonful or two of your chosen loose tea into the teabag and draw it tight. You may need a gentle knot to keep it closed while your tea brews.

MORE SCENT

Turn your teabags into lavender bags by topping them up with dried lavender instead of tea. Make sure you double-bow your drawstrings really tight as you don't want lavender falling out all over your knicker drawer. Replace the cotton thread with 5 mm (¼ inch) wide ribbon for a glamorous look – touch the cut ends with clear nail varnish to prevent fraying.

VINTAGE STAR

Sparkly head-gear never goes out of fashion, but this little wonder unashamedly champions the glitz and glamour of Twenties' film stars. Channel Clara Bow or Louise Brooks with some red lips and this little sparkler embedded in your chic bob or Marcel-waved curls – or make it for your vintage-loving pal. If you're giving it as a present, don't forget to add some seriously glam wrapping and tissue paper for that jewels-on-the-dressing-table look.

All you will need are a couple of pots of sequins and some soft faux leather – I used oddments from a disintegrated handbag lining.

MATERIALS

- ⁕ Hair clasp
- ⁕ Matching sewing thread
- ⁕ Scraps of faux leather
- ⁕ Sequins – silver star-shaped flat sequins/copper and blue cup sequins

EQUIPMENT

- ⁕ PVA glue
- ⁕ Scissors
- ⁕ Sewing needle

SEWING ON SEQUINS

The easiest way to sew on sequins is to bring up your needle through the faux leather where you want the centre of the sequin to be. Thread on a sequin and push it down flat to the material. Now make a tiny stitch to the right, bringing the needle back down through the leather just at the edge of your sequin. Bring the needle up again slightly to the right of the stitch you have just made, and thread on another sequin. It should overlap the previous sequin, and cover up the stitch you made. Keep going!

WHAT TO DO

1. Draw two circles on the back of your faux leather. Mine were 7 cm (2¾ inches) in diameter – use compasses or a suitably-sized glass to draw around. Cut out.

2. Take one circle. The 'right' side will be the one that looks more shiny and leathery and you will stitch your sequins onto that. Begin with the star-shaped sequins and sew a row around the circumference of the circle. See the box on the left for tips.

3. Add another row of star sequins, overlapping the first.

4. With your next row, alternate star sequins with blue cup sequins. This will add to a graduated effect. Again, overlap as you go.

5. Add two rows of blue sequins.

6. Alternate blue and copper sequins for the next row.

7. The final rows will be entirely copper sequins. Pile them on top of each other to make sure all the faux leather is covered. Finish the thread on the wrong side of the leather with a few stitches in place.

ALTERNATIVES

You – or your glamorous friend – may prefer a more 1950s or burlesque look. To make a 1950s-style pancake hat, increase the diameter of the faux-leather circles to about 12 cm (4 ¾ inches). To fill up the extra space more quickly, use pailette sequins (the large flat kind with a single hole at the top). Instead of using a hair clasp, use a plastic comb or alligator clip and stitch firmly in place.

Alternatively, for a more daytime look, use coiled rick-rack braid or ruffled ribbon stitched to a felt circle to decorate your leather circle. You could even glue pretty scraps of paper or cut-out fabric motifs for a découpage look.

Or add a long, curving feather or two and you have a fascinator for a wedding.

TO FINISH

1. Add some glue to the back of your circle and to the wrong side of the remaining circle. Press the two wrong sides together. This will cover up all your stitches and make your hair clasp really sturdy.

2. While the glue is still drying, glue your clasp to the back of the circle, making sure it is in the centre. If there are holes in your clasp, add some stitches for extra firmness.

3. Let your ornament dry. I placed mine sequin-side up and held my hand over the top for a few minutes. This meant that as the glue dried, the warmth of my hand helped the faux-leather mould over the clasp into a slightly convex shape, which makes it sit more easily on the head.

4. Once the hair slide is dry (give it a few hours or overnight) whip it into your curls, add a Manhattan and get your Charleston on!

BRACE YOURSELF

All you need to make these bracelets are old T-shirts and some imagination. Both soft and light, they could be easily popped in the envelope with a birthday card as a little gift.

They're also easily customisable – go for a plain braid in a neutral colour for your fashionista friends, add wooden beads for a boho look, weave in sequin strands for added glamour or mix and match patterned T-shirts with plain, or plait different-coloured fabric for a grown-up friendship bracelet.

You could even go for the grunge by splashing your finished bangles with bleach (wear rubber gloves and use an old toothbrush) and leaving them in the sun for some '90s edge.

I personally love the pink pony beads (got to love pink and black!) because they remind me of my days as a (faux) skatepunk boasting at least 20 bracelets on each wrist. But that's just my embarrassing past; you don't have to go there.

MATERIALS

✳ Beads/ribbons, sequin strands, etc
✳ Matching sewing thread
✳ Old T-shirts

EQUIPMENT

✳ Scissors
✳ Sewing needle

MAKING THE STRANDS

Cut strips horizontally across your T-shirt, about 2 cm (¾ inch) wide, cutting them to just short of the side seams. Take each end of a strip between finger and thumb and stretch it gently. The edges should curl in, creating a lovely soft strand with no raw edges.

1. BEADY

For this bracelet, cut four strands from a black T-shirt – make them slightly narrower than above. Thread three with a selection of plastic pony beads. Wrap the three strands around your wrist to work out how big you want the bracelet, then tie them together in a tight knot and trim the ends. Use the fourth strand to bind around the other three strands – wind around several times, covering the knot, and finish with another knot. Trim any loose ends, and stitch the strand in place.

2. PUTTING ON THE GLITZ

Cut three strands from your T-shirt. I added a piece of ribbon next to one strand, and a string of sequins next to another, and sewed the ends together as before. Plait until the bracelet reaches sufficient length. Fasten, trim and fix in a circle before covering up the ends as before – but use a narrower strip as this bracelet is much daintier.

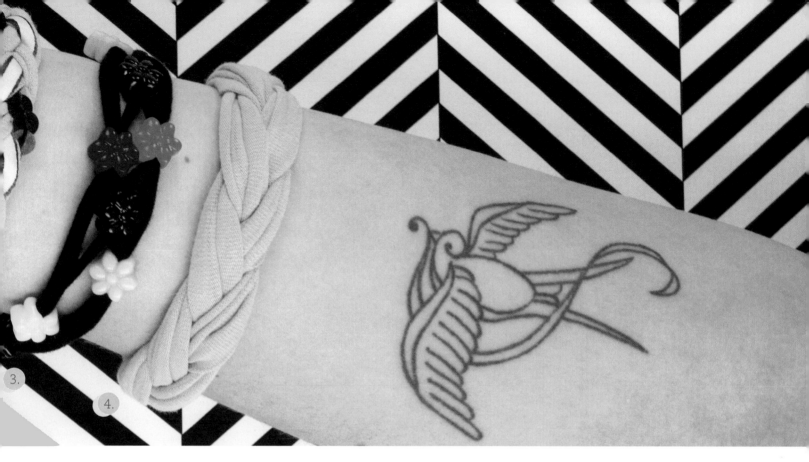

3. ZIGZAG

Again cut four thin strands from a black T-shirt. Arrange next to each other; it may help to hold the ends down with a heavy object or with some masking tape on the table top. Thread the strands through some plastic flower beads in a net pattern as in the diagram below.

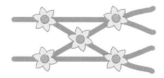

Once the bracelet is long enough, knot and trim the excess ends. Cut another strand from the T-shirt and, as before, wrap tightly around the knotted ends of the bracelet and stitch in place.

4. BRAIDY BUNCH

Thread your needle with a matching sewing thread and loosely sew six strands of fabric next to each other at one end, keeping them flat. Divide into three pairs and plait. Once it is long enough to go loosely around a wrist, pinch the strands in one hand and sew them loosely together. Snip off the excess lengths. Layer one end of the bracelet over the other and stitch both together. Now cut a strip about 5 cm x 8 cm (2 inches x 3⅛ inches) and tug it gently lengthways so the edges curl in. Wrap it around your bracelet to cover up the stitching. Tuck the raw ends in on the underside of the bracelet and stitch closed with small whip stitches (see p. 14).

Depart Heathrow
14·27
Arrive Berlin
16·45
Call Anna if
Problems xx

I have lost a white
sock. Have you
seen it?
Lots of love
♥

Hotel de la
Reine
475 Rue
Montmartre
PARIS

- apples
- oranges
- chilli
- couscous
- milk

Please feed the
cat for me
THANKS

L Hello

247 x 198

Milk

2.
get your craft on

BOSSY TEA TOWELS

Flatmate won't wash up? Boyfriend/girlfriend ignoring the teetering pile in the sink? It's time to get bossy! These tea towels are perfectly pretty but will also gently cajole your roomies into getting their paws on those dirty plates.

Make one or two and wrap them around a bottle of wine/tin of cupcakes as a sweet bribe for your hygienically challenged pals – or whizz up some matching tea towels as a present for newlyweds or a couple who have just moved in together. Add your recipients' names and I guarantee they'll use them . . .

MATERIALS

* Bobble trim
* Embroidery thread
* Iron-on Bondaweb or similar
* Scraps of patterned cotton
* Sewing thread (you can match or clash)
* Tough cotton fabric, 39 cm x 54 cm (15⅜ inches x 21¼ inches) per tea towel

EQUIPMENT

* Cotton wool
* Embroidery needle
* Iron and ironing board
* Paper
* Pins
* Scissors
* Sewing machine (optional)
* Sewing needle
* Water soluble fabric marker pen

MAKING THE TEA TOWEL

1. Press your fabric and decide which side will be the right (i.e. visible) side. Place it right side down.

2. Fold over one long edge 1 cm (⅜ inch) onto the wrong side and press. Fold over another 1 cm (⅜ inch) and press. Pin in place and sew with a straight stitch all along the inner folded edge. Take out the pins.

3. Do the same on the other long edge.

4. Repeat on the two short edges of the tea towel. Press everything again.

MAKING YOUR LETTERS

You could use a stencil to ensure all of your letters are the same size but I think this way is far more idiosyncratic and personal.

1. Cut a rectangle of paper the size you want each letter to be as a template. Mine was about 5.5 cm x 9 cm (2⅛ inches x 3½ inches) but cut yours to suit your tea towel and the number of letters you will need to spell out your message.

2. Using the template, cut out enough rectangles from the flowery fabric to make all the letters you will need – it ensures that they are all approximately the same size.

3. Use a pen to sketch out each letter on each rectangle. It may help to practise on paper first. If you are repeating a letter, use the first one as a template for the others.

4. Now cut out all your letters. Use them as a template to cut out the equivalent letters in Bondaweb.

ADDING THE MESSAGE

1. If your tea towel fabric is plain, use a ruler and fabric pen to mark out straight lines to place your words on.

2. It may help to fold the tea towel in half lengthways, press firmly along the crease, and then open up. This will help you place your letters equally on either side of the halfway mark.

3. Once you are sure, place each Bondaweb letter, with the fabric letter on top, in place on the tea towel and press on. It is easier to do one word at a time.

FINISHING OFF

1. Now your letters are in place, you want them to look pretty. Thread your embroidery needle with two strands of embroidery thread and knot the end. Starting at the outside corner of each letter, use blanket stitch (see p. 15) around the outer edges of your first letter. Then finish off around any inside edges.

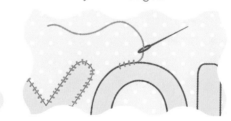

1.

2. Continue along each letter until you have outlined all your letters. Try to keep the back of the tea towel as neat as you can, as you don't want your trailing strands getting caught on the washing up! Use several stitches in place to finish off each line of blanket stitch.

3. Last of all, cut two 37 cm (14⅝ inches) lengths of bobble trim. Pin each one in place along the short edges of the tea towel, folding the raw ends over twice on the wrong side of the tea towel. Stitch in place by hand using a needle and thread and a small straight stitch (see p. 15).

HEY, FOUR EYES!

When I was a short-sighted 13-year-old, dorky specs were the last thing I wanted to be wearing (especially as I had braces too – far too much metal for one face). Nowadays anyone who's anyone wears glasses – and they're going to need somewhere to put them.

These cases are easy to whip up for yourself or your myopic pal and will keep your spectacles scratch-free.

MATERIALS:

- ✳ Good quality white cotton/cotton drill, 16 cm x 20 cm (6¼ inches x 8 inches)
- ✳ Matching sewing thread
- ✳ Popper
- ✳ Printed cotton, 16 cm x 20 cm (6¼ inches x 8 inches)
- ✳ Scrap of felt
- ✳ Sequins

EQUIPMENT

- ✳ Fabric glue (if required)
- ✳ Iron and ironing board
- ✳ Pins
- ✳ Scissors
- ✳ Sewing machine
- ✳ Sewing needle
- ✳ Water soluble fabric marker pen (if required)

HOW TO MAKE IT

1. Press your two rectangles of fabric. Place them right sides together – this is the side with the pattern or the smoothest surface. Plain white cotton is usually the same both sides. Pin together.

2. With your sewing machine, or by hand, stitch around the four sides, about 5 mm (¼ inch) from the raw edges. Leave a gap of about 5 cm (2 inches) on one edge.

3. Trim the four raw corners off the rectangle, taking care not to cut through the stitches. This removes any bulk at the corners of your glasses case.

4. Turn the rectangle right side out through the gap. Use a chopstick, knitting needle or other pointed instrument to poke the corners out. Press flat, tucking in the raw edges of the gap.

5. Use whip stitch (see p. 14) to close the hole and then press.

6. Now make your glasses shape! I went for a 1950s ladies' cat's eye shape and a sharp 1960s man's spectacle design – very *Mad Men* – but feel free to sketch your own. Just draw one half on a piece of folded paper, so the bridge of the glasses is at the fold, then cut out through both sides – to make sure your glasses are symmetrical. Make sure the overall size is about 17 cm x 5 cm (6¾ inches x 2 inches).

7. Use the pattern to cut out the glasses shape from the felt. If you are making the ladies' cat's eye glasses, stitch a flower-shaped sequin in each of the top corners. You could go crazy with the decorations – add more sequins, embroidery, beads and other sparkles. For cool cats, make the frames out of black felt and cut out shapes, slightly larger than the lenses, from dark grey felt. Glue them to the back of the frames – *et voila, sunglasses!*

8. Fold your rectangle in half lengthways, so that the patterned fabric is on the inside and the fold is along the top. Pin together. Place your glasses shape in the correct position on the white rectangle and pin in place through the top layer only. Take out the other pins and open the rectangle out again.

8.

9. For extra safety, tack the glasses shape to the fabric using contrasting-coloured cotton thread so it is easy to remove afterwards. Using your sewing machine, or hand stitching, sew the glasses shape to the white side of the rectangle, following the outside and inside edges of the shape. Remove the pins and tacking.

10. Fold the rectangle in half lengthways again and pin. Use whip stitch to sew the long edges and left-hand short edges together. Stitch through the protruding patterned cotton, not the white. This will be neater, and give a 'sandwich' look to your glasses case.

11. Nearly there! Open your popper and sew each half to the inside of your case, just inside the opening.

TEMPLATE: ACTUAL SIZE

MAKE A POLISHING CLOTH

For an extra personal touch, cut a rectangle about 15 cm x 8 cm (6 inches x 3¹⁄₁₆ inches) from an old duster or moleskin cotton. Hem the edges using two strands of embroidery thread and blanket stitch (see p. 15). Write your friend's initial in fabric pen and embroider over the top using stem stitch (see p. 15). Blot away the pen marks with damp cotton wool.

Tuck inside the glasses case.

PET PROJECT

Rented flats and cats don't mix – but get round the killjoy rules of landlords with these lifelike cuddly cushions.

Use photographs of your friend's dog or cat to make them a personal pet cushion – or download free images from the internet for the truly animal-deprived. There's no need to stick to pets either – use a photograph of yourself to make a rather stalker-esque cushion for distant friends (who needs Skype?) or make your pal a handy punch bag with a photo of her scumbag ex.

MATERIALS

- A3 paper
- Buttons/ribbon
- Matching sewing thread
- Toy stuffing
- White cotton, two pieces each about 40 cm x 30 cm (15¾ inches x 12 inches) depending on how big you want your cushion

EQUIPMENT

- Computer and printer
- Dylan Image Maker or similar
- Iron and ironing board
- Kitchen towel
- Newspaper
- Old brush
- Scissors
- Sewing machine
- Sewing needle
- Superglue
- Sponge

WHAT TO DO

1. Choose your image! You will need a large high-resolution photographic image (around 300 dpi) of your animal on a white background. Remember: during the following process it will come out as a mirror-image unless you reverse it in Photoshop or a similar programme now!

2. Print out the photograph using colour ink onto the white A3 paper. Cut out, leaving a border about 1 cm (⅜ inch) around the edge of your image. Make sure the bottom edge is a flat line. Lay it on some newspaper.

3. Press your pieces of cotton fabric. Choose one to be the front of your cushion and lay it flat on more newspaper.

4. Pour squiggles of Image Maker onto the printed side of your image and spread thickly and evenly with the brush. Before it dries, carefully pick up the paper and press it wet-side down onto your fabric. Use a bunched-up piece of kitchen towel to smooth it down and to soak up any excess.

5. Now leave to dry according to the manufacturer's instructions – for a minimum of four hours. If you're impatient, leaving it on a central heating radiator can speed up the process, but make sure it's lying flat.

6. Once it's dry, lay your fabric on the newspaper again and using, a damp sponge, gently scrub at the paper. It should come off easily, leaving your design transferred to the fabric. Leave to dry again.

7. Once your fabric is dry, the image will probably still be unclear so repeat the process with the damp sponge to remove the final pieces of paper. Allow to dry. Add a final thin layer of Image Maker to seal the image.

8. Place your fabric image-side down onto the other piece of fabric and pin together. Using your sewing machine (or if you are sewing by hand, a small, neat, back stitch (see p. 13) sew around the image, leaving a hem about 3 cm (1⅛ inches) wide. Follow the shape all the way round, leaving a gap of 5 cm (2 inches) on the straight bottom edge.

9. Trim off excess fabric, following the shape you have just stitched, leaving a small allowance.

10. Turn the cushion right side out through the gap you left. The fabric will be quite stiff so use a ruler or chopstick to poke out the corners of the shape.

11. Now stuff your cushion with the toy stuffing. Use the ruler or chopstick again to pack it in firmly.

12. Once your cushion is full, tuck in the raw edges of the gap and whip stitch (see p. 14) to close.

13. Add some decorations! This is where your stash comes in handy – use a ribbon bow, button, beads or even a bell on some ribbon and superglue them in place. The more ridiculous the better!

A HOTTIE FOR MY HOTTIE

I'm an old-fashioned girl at heart and, although an electric blanket is a necessity through a frosty winter, I've rented enough icy flats to know that filling a hot water bottle for your roomie on a cold night is just another way of saying 'I love you'.

This fleecy hot water bottle cover is just one step further – kitschy colours, pretty ribbon and pompoms – what else could your chilly chum ask for? Of course you could strip it back without any embellishments for the conservative chap in your life who buys everything from Muji – but where's the fun in that?

The back of this hottie cover tucks closed with a simple flap, but if you are worried about movement, add some squares of Velcro to keep things snug.

MATERIALS

* Fleece, 50 cm x 50 cm (19¾ inches x 19¾ inches)
* Matching sewing thread
* Patterned cotton fabric, 50 cm x 50 cm (19¾ inches x 19¾ inches)
* Ribbon
* Yarn

EQUIPMENT

* An empty hot water bottle
* Cardboard
* Pins
* Ruler
* Scissors
* Sewing machine or sewing needle
* Yarn needle

WHAT TO DO

1. Photocopy the template on p. 65, increasing by 200 per cent. Or make a pattern by laying the hottie on some newspaper and tracing around it, then adding a 2 cm (¾ inch) seam allowance. Cut out three patterns.

2. Use one pattern to cut out one shape from the fleece and one from your pattern lining. Set aside.

3. Grab another pattern piece, and mark out a line horizontally across about one third of the way down from the top. Mine was about 17 cm (6¾ inches) from the top. As long as it is below the 'shoulders' of the bottle shape, you will be fine. Cut across, and discard the smaller half of the pattern. Use the remaining piece to cut out one shape from the fleece and one from the pattern lining. Set aside.

4. Grab the last pattern piece and mark out a line about 5 cm (2 inches) lower than last time. Cut across and discard the larger piece of pattern. Use the smaller piece to cut out one shape from the fleece, and one from the pattern lining. Set aside.

THE FRONT

1. Return to your two largest HWB shapes and give them a good press. Match them up so the patterned side of the lining and the smoother side of the fleece are facing each other. Pin. Stitch the two shapes together using a straight stitch on your machine or by hand, using back stitch (see p. 13) leaving a 1 cm (⅜ inch) hem. Leave a gap of about 5 cm (2 inches) on one side. Snip the outer curves of your piece

2. Turn your shape right side out through the gap. Poke the curves out using a pencil or chopstick. Press your shape flat, folding in the raw edges of the gap you left. Whip stitch it closed (see p. 14).

RIBBON

1. Trim the end of your ribbon neatly, and fold the raw edge under. Press. Place it horizontally across your bottle shape. Make sure your ribbon meets the opposite seam on the front of the HWB cover, add about 3 mm (⅛ inch) and trim. Fold under, press. Pin in place.

2. Make sure your sewing thread matches the base colour of your ribbon. Handstitch the ribbon to your bottle cover using two lines of straight stitch (see p. 15) near the top and bottom of your ribbon.

THE BOTTOM BACK PIECE

1. Grab the two pieces which will make the bottom part of the back of your HWB cover. Press. Match them up so the patterned side of the lining and the smoother side of the fleece are facing each other. Pin. Stitch the two shapes together using a straight stitch on your machine or by hand, leaving a 1 cm (⅜ inch) hem. Leave a gap of about 5 cm (2 inches) on one side. Snip the curves.

2. Turn your shape through the gap to the right side. Poke the curves out using a pencil or chopstick. Press your shape flat, folding in the raw edges of the gap you left. Whip stitch it closed.

THE TOP BACK PIECE

1. Get the two pieces which will make the top part of the back of your HWB. Press. Match them up so the patterned side of the lining and the smoother side of the fleece are facing each other. Pin. Stitch the two shapes together using a straight stitch on your machine or by hand, leaving a 1 cm (⅜ inch) hem. Leave a gap of about 5 cm (2 inches) on one side. Snip the curves.

2. As before, turn your shape through the gap to the right side. Poke the curves out using a pencil or chopstick. Press your shape flat, folding in the raw edges of the gap you left. Whip stitch it closed.

3. Now you have the three lovely plump, lined pieces of your HWB cover!

HOW TO MAKE A POMPOM

You can buy fancy plastic pompom makers these days but I prefer the old cardboard circle version my Nanny Rita showed me.

You will need some relatively thin cardboard (massacring a cereal packet is your best bet). Work out how big you want your pompom and either draw a circle of the same circumference on the cardboard using a compass, or wing it and find a bottle or wine glass with a round bottom of a pleasing size (don't we all want one of those!).

Draw another circle and cut both out.

Find the middle of each circle (your compass comes in useful here) and cut out a hole – make its diameter about a fifth of the diameter of your circle (so 1 cm (⅜ inch) for a 5 cm (2 inch) pompom. It doesn't have to be neat. Place the two circles together.

Now cut a long length of yarn, pass one end through the hole in the middle of your cardboard doughnut and either tie a knot, or tuck it under the yarn as you start to wind. Wind your yarn firmly round and round your doughnut shape.

Keep your wrapping as even as possible. When you run out of yarn, cut another long piece and tuck it under as you wind round.

Keep going until you can't pass the yarn through the hole any more. Then thread yarn on a bodkin (a big, blunt needle) and keep going until the centre hole is full.

Holding it all firmly, line your scissors up where you think the two cardboard edges of your circles are under all that yarn. Snip through the yarn all around the circumference of the circle.

Once you're done, cut a longish bit of yarn and tuck it between the two cardboard circles. Pull it round and knot. Knot once more, and once more, for security. Now pull off the cardboard circles – you may have to tear or cut them to get them loose.

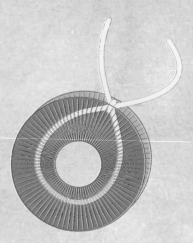

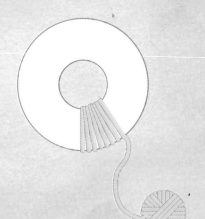

Et voila! Fluff up your pompom and trim any rogue long pieces

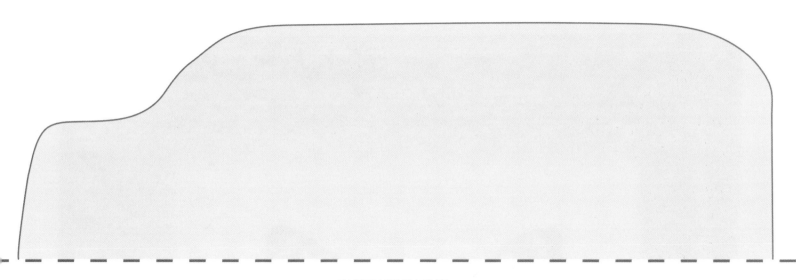

INCREASE BY 200%

ALL TOGETHER NOW

1. Lay your front piece down, fleecy side up. Place the bottom back piece on top, fleecy side down. Pin. Stitch together down one side of the back piece, along the bottom, and up the other side, leaving the smallest possible seam allowance.

2. Now lay the top back piece in place, fleecy side down. It should overlap your bottom piece by about 5 cm (2 inches). Pin. Stitch together in the same way, but start just above where your top piece overlaps the bottom, and finish in the same place on the other side. Don't stitch all three layers together!

3. Turn your HWB cover right side out, and poke the corners with a pencil or chopstick. press flat. Tuck the top back piece inside the bottom back piece.

POMPOMS

1. First make the little channel for the pompom string to go through. Cut four small rectangles from fleece and pin to the neck of your HWB cover, two in front, two on the back. Hand stitch in place. Take out the pins.

2. Make two pompoms of 5 cm (2 inches) diameter from your yarn (see opposite).

3. Now make the string they go on. Cut three lengths of yarn, two 65 cm (25⅝ inches) long and one 80 cm (31½ inches) long. Place them so that the longer one is in the middle, extending about 7 cm (2¾ inches) each end of the shorter ones. Knot close to the top of the shorter strands.

4. Plait the three pieces. It's easier to tape to a table or, if you don't mind a bit of fluff in your mouth, just hold one end in your teeth. Again knot near the end of the shorter pieces.

5. Finally, attach the pompoms. Thread your string through the front right rectangle, through the back rectangles and out through the front left rectangle. Thread the long strand at one end of your string onto your yarn needle and poke it through the centre of one of the pompoms. Stitch through several times until you are sure it is secure. Trim any excess yarn. Attach the other pompom to the end as before.

Pull gently to gather the neck of your HWB cover and tie in a bow and you are done!

 **reading is sexy**

GOFFRATA

SHIP

GO TO BED EYES . . .

Living in the city, it's pretty hard to get a good night's sleep – if it's not the street lights keeping you awake, it's the frequent emergency services flashing past. Block them all out with one of these silky eye masks.

The sequinned version would make a perfect present for the glamazon who needs her beauty sleep; make two and embroider them 'his' and 'hers' for any insomniac couples you know – or make yourself one with an offensive message on it to get rid of bothersome types who want to keep you awake. Sometimes a gal's just got to sleep.

MATERIALS

- Black lining material, 30 cm x 20 cm (12 inches x 8 inches)
- 5 cm (2 inch) wide elastic (you will need enough to go halfway round your head)
- Embroidery thread
- Matching sewing thread
- Rick-rack braid/lace/sequins
- Satin, 30 cm x 20 cm (12 inches x 8 inches)
- White cotton/cotton drill, 30 cm x 20 cm (12 inches x 8 inches)

EQUIPMENT

- Cotton wool
- Embroidery/sewing needles
- Iron and ironing board
- Pencil or chopstick
- Pins
- Sewing machine, if necessary
- Scissors
- Water soluble fabric marker pen

BEFORE YOU START

1. First press your three pieces of fabric. Make a template from the one opposite with some tracing paper or fine white paper. Simply fold your paper in half, line up the fold of the paper with the straight line of the template and trace around the shape with a pencil. Keeping it folded, cut out. Open up and pin the template to your white cotton and cut round it. Do the same with the satin and the lining.

GET DESIGNING

1. Of course you don't need to add any decorations at all – use colourful fabric instead of the white cotton and let the pattern do the talking. Or make it in black for a Zorro look. I like to add as much sparkle as possible to any project so I went for two designs – a sleeping prima donna and a simple embroidered message. I opted for the PG version ('go away') but something a bit sterner may be in order if you really cherish your Zs.

2. The eyes – hold your white eye mask shape over your face where it is likely to rest and use your fabric pen to dot where the bumps of your (closed!) eyes are. This will help you place your embroidery.

3. Now draw on the eyelids and the eyebrows. If you're not too sure of your drawing skills, practise on a bit of paper first with a felt tip. Once you've got your design right, lay

the eye mask shape over the top and trace the design with your fabric pen.

4. Thread your embroidery needle with two strands of black embroidery thread and back stitch (see p. 13) to hold it in place. Beginning at the outside corner of one eyelid, chain stitch (see p. 14) along to the inside corner. Thread your thread through to the wrong side and come up again about 5 mm (¼ inch) along the eyelid. Make a single chain stitch, this time facing downwards. Bring the needle up about 5 mm (¼ inch) further along the eyelid and add another downward chain stitch. Work your way along, making longer stitches at the middle of the eye and shortening at each end. The eyebrows are single lines of chain stitch, working from the outer corner inwards.

5. Once you're done, blot away the fabric pen with damp cotton wool. Use sewing thread to stitch on a couple of sequins.

GO AWAY!

1. As before, place the mask over your face to mark out the position of your eyes. Draw your message straight onto the fabric with the fabric pen, centring it over the dots, or, like before, sketch it out on paper first and trace through the fabric.

2. Neat, handwriting-style letters work well with chain stitch, although you could go with capital letters if you really want to get your message across. Just remember that too long a word or message will curve across your face, so the beginning and end letters may get lost.

I used two strands of black embroidery thread, although any strong colour would look good. Again, dab away your pen marks when you're done.

TEMPLATE: ACTUAL SIZE

PAPER FOLD

MAKE YOUR MASK

1. Now that your eye mask looks smoking hot, give it a quick press as it's probably got crumpled in your hands. Now it's time to assemble your masterpiece.

2. Stack your cut-out eye mask shapes in this order – the satin piece, with its right side (the silky, patterned side) facing up. Then your white piece with the embroidery, facing downwards. Then your black piece. Pin together.

3. Sew around the edge of the shape either with a straight stitch on your machine or with back stitch by hand, leaving a 5 mm (¼ inch) seam allowance. Leave a 5 cm (2 inch) gap on the bottom edge.

4. Snip the outer curves with small sharp scissors, being careful not to cut your stitching. This will remove the bulk and make it easier to have a nice curved shape.

5. Turn your eye mask shape right side out through the gap you left. Ensure that the white piece is at the front, and the right side of the satin facing out at the back. The black lining should be hidden inside.

6. Use something pointy like a pencil or chopstick to poke out the curves of your eye mask from the inside. Press flat, tucking in the raw edges of the gap you left. Sew it together using whip stitch (see p. 14).

TO FINISH

1. Add the finishing touch to your eye mask with a line of rick-rack braid or lace stitched around the outer edge.

2. Now pin your elastic to one side of the eye mask, hold the mask against your eyes and loop the elastic round your head to the other side of the mask. Once it feels like it fits (but isn't tight), pin the other end in place. Take off the mask and carefully remove one pin, not letting the elastic spring away. Fold over the raw end twice and hand stitch it to the back of your mask. Do the same at the other end of your elastic.

VARIATION

For a seductive touch, use two long lengths of silk ribbon instead of elastic, and tie in a bow. Ooh la la!

TOTES AWESOME

Tote bags are super easy projects and make great presents – because who hasn't got stuff to carry? Plus, hopefully, we've all got the news that cramming our wares into a plastic bag is the opposite of eco-friendly – and the opposite of stylish.

This tote bag is strong enough to carry your shopping, while the punky studs add a bit of bling. The pattern is easily amended to spell out your friend's name – or any other word they tend to say a lot. (If you decide to use a swear word, don't blame me if people on the bus get offended.)

MATERIALS

- ✻ Black cotton drill, 42 cm x 38 cm (16½ inches x 15 inches) for the bag and two pieces, 20 cm x 60 cm (8 inches x 23⅝ inches) for the handles
- ✻ 150 gold claw studs, around 1 cm (⅜ inch) in width
- ✻ Matching sewing thread

EQUIPMENT

- ✻ Dressmaker's chalk
- ✻ Iron and ironing board
- ✻ Pencil or chopstick
- ✻ Pins
- ✻ Ruler
- ✻ Scissors
- ✻ Sewing machine
- ✻ Sewing needles

MAKING THE BAG

1. Hem each short side of your bag – fold over 1 cm (⅜ inch) onto the wrong side (cotton drill doesn't really have a wrong side, but for our purposes, I mean the side you don't want to be seen).

2. Press with a hot iron. Fold over another 1 cm (⅜ inch), press and stitch along the bottom folded edge. Repeat on the other short side.

TO DO THE STUDS

1. Lay your fabric flat, with the right side upwards and a short side facing you.

2. Pull the fabric towards you until half is hanging off the table. The half left behind on the table will be the front of your bag.

3. Using a ruler, measure down 10 cm (4 inches) from the top edge of the fabric and draw a line across with dressmaker's chalk. Draw another line across 8 cm (3⅛ inches) below that. Complete the rectangle with vertical lines each side, 2 cm (¾ inch) in from the edges.

4. If you want to spell out 'Totes', copy my design opposite using the chalk.

   To create your own design, lay your claw studs out on the table to work out the letter shapes. Don't forget to leave a gap between each letter. And make sure your message doesn't exceed 34 cm (13⅛ inches) across or it will get caught up in the seams of your tote.

5. Press each stud into place, folding the little legs over on the wrong side of the fabric. Try to use a tough implement such as a pencil or chopstick to fold the legs in otherwise you will wreck your nails. They don't have to be in perfect lines. Use a 'brickwork' pattern for shapes which have a curve to them, such as Ss and Es.

TIP

If you are finding the chalk a faff, mark out your word on tracing paper using a black felt-tip. Then pin it to your fabric. You can push the studs through the paper and then rip it away when you've finished.

1.

3.

TOTES!

INCREASE BY 200%

TO COMPLETE THE BAG

1. Once your message is complete, bring up the fabric hanging off the table and fold it over to match the two hemmed top edges. This means the right sides of the fabric are facing each other.

2. Pin in place, then on your sewing machine sew down each side, leaving a 1 cm (⅜ inch) seam allowance. Using a zigzag stitch, sew down each rough edge of the fabric, to prevent fraying.

3. Fold the bag the right way out and press with your iron.

2.

TO MAKE THE HANDLES

1. Take one piece of handle fabric, fold it in half lengthways and press. Open out. Fold the long edges into the fold line you have made and press. Then fold in half again along the original fold line. Press.

2. Sew along the open edge of your handle, then back down the folded edge. Fold under each raw end 1 cm (⅜ inch) and press. Repeat for the other handle.

3. Pin each end of the handles in place on the inside of the bag. You want to position them 6 cm (2⅜ inches) in from each edge and about 5 cm (2 inches) down inside the bag.

4. Make sure the raw edges are tucked in between each handle and the inside of the bag. Sew in place, going along the short end first. Stitching a rectangle on each handle end will keep your handles strong.

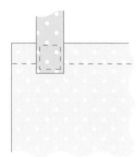

CLAW IT BACK

If, like me, you go a bit OTT when buying the claw studs, don't let them sit, all sad, in your stash box. They would look cool on a 90s-style denim jacket, down the sides of a skirt, or to decorate your Converse. You could even use some strips of faux leather and a popper to knock up some studded bracelets, 80s rocker style.

BUTTON UP

I didn't think the world needed any more laptop/tablet/phone covers until I saw a man carrying his phone in a sock – a *sock*.

This design is simple to make and can be adapted to fit any size of device – just adjust the measurements. It also recycles an old shirt, which means there's no need for zips, Velcro or any other fastenings, and the felt lining and the chunky seams protect the precious device inside.

Make one for your techy loved-one; but perhaps ask first before you cut up their favourite shirt!

MATERIALS

* An old shirt
* Felt
* Matching sewing thread

EQUIPMENT

* Iron and ironing board
* Newspaper
* Pencil
* Ruler
* Scissors
* Sewing machine

WHAT TO DO

1. First measure the width and height of your device – it may help to look online for the manufacturer's exact measurements. Add about 1 cm (½ inch) to each measurement to account for the depth of the device, plus 1 cm (⅜ inch) each side for a seam allowance.

2. Draw this rectangle onto newspaper and cut out as a template.

3. Place the buttoned-up shirt on your ironing board and give it a good press. Place it so that the ironing board is through the middle of the shirt and the buttoned side is on top of the board.

4. Fold your template in half lengthways and place it on the shirt so that the fold line as adjacent to the centre of the buttons. Make sure your buttons will be placed squarely on your device cover and are not falling off the ends. Open the template again carefully and pin in place.

5. Cut out the rectangle and press – this will be the front of your device cover.

6. Remove the pins and use your template to cut out another rectangle from a buttonless part of the shirt, probably the back. This will be the back of your device cover. Take out the pins and press.

7. Use the template to cut another piece from felt. Remove the pins and press.

MAKING THE BACK

1. Place your fabric back piece right side (patterned side) up, with the felt piece on top. Pin in place.

2. Sew around the four sides leaving a 5 mm (¼ inch) seam allowance. Leave a small gap on one side. Trim off the four corners, being careful not to snip the stitching.

3. Remove the pins and turn your piece around the right way through the gap. Use a pointy object such as a pencil or chopstick to poke out the corners.

4. Press your rectangle, tucking in the raw edges of the gap. Sew closed.

MAKING THE FRONT

1. Take your front piece and unbutton it so you have two halves. Lay one aside for the moment.

2. Take your remaining shirt half and pin it to your felt. Use it as a template to cut out a matching rectangle of felt. Take out the pins.

3. Turn your shirt piece over so the wrong side is facing upwards. Place the felt piece on top, tucking it under the placket (the piece of cloth which reinforces the button/buttonhole areas on a shirt) until it lines up against the buttonholes or stitches for the buttons. Pin in place.

4. Trim off any excess felt.

5. Stitch along the bottom edge of the rectangle you have made, leaving a 5 mm (¼ inch) seam allowance, then up the long side (not the one with the buttons/buttonholes) and along the top edge. Fasten off.

6. Turn your piece the right way round, poke out the corners with your chopstick and press flat.

7. Finish the piece by sewing down the line of the placket edge.

8. Repeat on the other shirt half.

ASSEMBLING

1. Place the back piece in front of you, felt side down. Button together the two shirt pieces and place the front piece on top, felt sides up. Pin in place.

2. Starting 5 cm (2 inches) from the corner, stitch together along the top edge towards the corner, leaving a 5 mm (¼ inch) seam allowance. Continue down the long side, and then another 5 cm (2 inches) along the bottom edge.

3. Repeat on the other side.

4. Unbutton the cover and turn it around the right way. Give it another press.

5. Pop your device inside, button up, and you're ready to go!

3.
crafty
minx

SQUASHY SISTERS

For me, craft and feminism go hand in hand (see p. 8) – and these cushion covers, as well as being practical, bright and pleasingly kitsch, celebrate some of the sassiest sisters in our history.

Made from felt and all the fun bits from your stash, these ladies are easily customisable so you can create your own icons – have a look at my list overleaf. I want a Dolly Parton cushion so badly! The cushions would make the perfect present for anyone who appreciates a little hussy in their homeware.

MATERIALS

* Beads/ribbon/patches/buttons/lace
* Coloured cotton/polycotton, 115 cm x 50 cm (45¼ inches x 19¾ inches)
* Cushion pad, 45 cm sq (17¾ inches)
* Matching sewing thread
* Various pieces of coloured felt, depending on your design
* White cotton/polycotton, 115 cm x 50 cm (45¼ inches x 19¾ inches)

EQUIPMENT

* Dressmaker's chalk
* Fabric glue
* Iron and ironing board
* Needles
* Paper
* Pencil or chopstick
* Pins
* Scissors
* Sewing machine
* Water soluble fabric marker pen

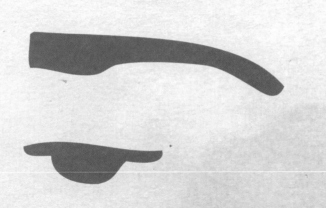

FRIDA

CARMEN

LADIES TO LOUNGE (ON)

Emmeline Pankhurst	Gloria Steinem	Amelia Earhart
Princess Leia	Florence Nightingale	Joan Jett
Rosie the Riveter	Virginia Woolf	Annie Lennox
Debbie Harry	Dolly Parton	Madonna
Missy Elliott	Angela Davis	Beth Ditto
Cleopatra	*Mad Men*'s Peggy Olsen	Your mum

NOSE!

PAM

LIZ

MAKING THE CUSHION COVER

These loose cushion covers are essentially a rectangle folded around, with one end tucked inside the other, so there is no need for zips or any other fastenings. Yay!

1. Press your white rectangle and coloured rectangle, and place one on top of the other. Pin in place. Sew around the four sides leaving a 1.5 cm (⅝ inch) seam allowance. Leave a gap of about 10 cm (4 inches) on one edge.

2. Cut off the four corners (being careful not to cut the stitching) and turn the cushion right side out through the gap. Poke the corners out with something pointy like a pencil or chopstick.

3. Press the rectangle flat, folding in the raw edges of the gap. Sew the gap closed.

MAKING YOUR LADY

1. Draw a template for the head and shoulders of your lady on a piece of paper. I drew a rough oval, approx 20 cm (8 inches) tall and 15 cm (6 inches) wide with a small neck and shoulders approx 20 cm (8 inches) wide. it doesn't have to be perfect! Cut out.

2. Press your felt and pin the template in place. Cut out.

3. Now it's time to make your lady's face. Copy my cushions on p. 91, or make your own by looking up photos of your lady online or in books.

Sketch an eye, eyebrow and nostril shape on to paper and cut out. If you need help, use my diagrams opposite. Use these as templates to cut out of black or brown felt – then turn the template over and cut out another set. Now is the time to trim your shapes to make them more idiosyncratic – Frida Kahlo had a mighty monobrow for example.

4. Fold a piece of paper in half and draw half a mouth on one side. Cut out, and use your symmetrical template to cut a mouth shape out of red or pink felt.

5. Assemble your pieces on the head-shaped piece of felt. Remember that eyes are actually located half-way down the head. Carefully tweak the angles of your pieces to adjust your lady's expression – one eyebrow higher than the other for a saucy minx, tilted eyes for a sad or in-charge look. Use pins to keep them in place until you are happy with the position, then fix with a little fabric glue.

   Hand sew the facial features in place with matching thread, then take out the pins.

6. Trim the sides of your head shape to make the face look more like your lady – she may have slimmer cheeks or a wonky hairline.

7. Choose a large piece of felt for the hair, place the head shape on top and pin in place. Sketch out the shape of the hair using dressmaker's chalk and cut out. If you are creating a fringe, cut out a forehead-sized piece from the hair-coloured felt, using the head piece as a template. Then place the hair on top of the head, and trim to the length you desire. Pin in place.

DECORATING

This is the fun bit – it's time to rummage through your stash for all the gaudiest, most glittery beads and ribbons you can find.

Frida Kahlo: Frida was known for her fabulous headgear, often influenced by traditional Mexican styles, and including flowers, head wraps and lots of gold jewellery. Use felt to create a 'headscarf', glue in place with fabric glue and appliqué around the edges. Make flowers from felt and from flowery fabric – pile up and attach in the same way. The necklace and earrings are made from gold bugle beads. Sew black felt triangles over the 'shoulder' pieces to suggest sleeves.

Elizabeth I: The queen used her clothes to emphasise her status as well as symbolising her famous virginity – use pale colours and lots of glitz. Gold seed beads decorate her hair and neck, while a string of 'pearls' suggests a crown. Pleated cream lace, stitched into place behind the 'neck' of the headpiece, works as a Tudor ruff.

Pam Grier: Scraps of red handkerchief, sewn into place with folded-down corners suggest a shirt. Pam also rocked an awesome afro – trim the edges with pinking shears – and use gold bugle beads to make hoop earrings.

Carmen Miranda: Carmen was famous for her giant headdresses. Make a base piece from green felt, then pile on your fruit and flowers. The glittery turquoise flowers were an appliqué design cut from an old T-shirt. The fruit was cut from scraps of felt and sewn on with large running stitches to suggest the segments and seeds. Add a handful of ribbon flowers (see the box opposite).

MAKING THE CUSHION

1. Place your cushion pad in the centre of your fabric rectangle, on the wrong (white) side. Fold the remaining fabric around it. The idea is that you are creating a tight envelope, with one side tucked under the other.

2. Once you feel that it is in the right place, pin it and mark with a fabric pen on the coloured AND the white cotton where the top piece of fabric rests on the under piece.

3. Turn the cushion over. Place your lady in the centre. Once you are sure of her position, pin her in place.

4. Turn the cushion over again, and take out all the pins.

5. Now it's time to sew your lady on. Using a 'skin'-coloured thread and zigzag stitch on the machine, follow around the outside shape of her head. Sew around the outside of her face. Remove the pins.

HOW TO MAKE RIBBON FLOWERS

Cut a length of ribbon, about 10 cm (4 inches) long.

Knot a piece of thread and stitch loosely but neatly along one edge of the ribbon.

When you reach the end, pull the thread and push gently on the ribbon so it gathers into a rosette shape. Stitch together through the centre, tucking in raw ends.

FINISHING THE CUSHION

1. Place the cushion cover piece right side up, and fold the two sides in as before but inside out. Match up the top flap with the marks you made before. Pin in place.

2. Now stitch along the top and bottom edges of your cushion cover, leaving a 1 cm (⅜ inch) seam allowance. Fasten off.

3. Turn your cushion cover the right way around, poking out the corners with a pencil or chopstick. Give it a good press.

4. Now stuff your cushion pad inside – it should be snug but moveable. And you're done!

CARMEN MIRANDA

Born in Portugal, actress Carmen Miranda grew up in Brazil and became synonymous with samba music and known for her fruity headdresses. An astute businesswoman as well as a superstar, she spent her life battling criticism for her apparent stereotyping of Latina women.

PAM GRIER

American actress Pam Grier is best known for her badass roles in Seventies blaxploitation flicks *Coffy* and *Foxy Brown* as well as in Tarantino's *Jackie Brown*. An action star when women were usually playing passive roles, she's a survivor both on and off screen.

ELIZABETH I

England's queen for nearly half a century, taking the throne when she was a mere 25, Elizabeth I is the ultimate symbol of female power and renowned for never marrying and thereby conceding her power to a man. Let's just draw a veil over all the executions, including that of her cousin Mary, Queen of Scots.

FRIDA KAHLO

Born in Mexico in 1907, artist Frida Kahlo struggled with terrible pain all her life from polio and a devastating bus accident – her surrealist paintings depicted women's suffering but were also beautiful and magical. Left-leaning politically, she had affairs with both men and women, including Trotsky, while enduring a tumultuous relationship with her husband, artist Diego Rivera. Plus check out the powerful eyebrows.

CLUTCH ME!

This faux leather clutch bag is perfect for parties and goes with everything from jeans and a T-shirt to vintage frocks. Make it for your stylish girlfriends – or it works equally well as a case for a laptop, iPad or e-reader. You could pop a real book in there too.

You will probably need a sewing machine for this one, as faux leather can be quite tough on the old fingers if you try to hand sew.

MATERIALS

- Faux leather, 43 cm x 62 cm (17 inches x 24½ inches)
- Patterned cotton for lining, 43 cm x 62 cm (17 inches x 24½ inches)
- 40 cm (15¾ inch) open-ended zip
- Sewing thread

EQUIPMENT

- Iron and ironing board
- Leather needle for your sewing machine
- Pencil or chopstick
- Pins
- Scissors
- Sewing machine
- Zip foot for your sewing machine

BEFORE YOU START

1. Put your iron on a low temperature and gently press the the non-leathery side of your faux leather. Turn the temperature up to hot and press your patterned cotton.

MAKE YOUR LINING

The lining fits inside the clutch like an extra bag, with the patterned side visible.

1. First, lay the fabric down, wrong side up (the duller side), with a short edge towards you. Take the other short edge and fold it over about 5 mm (¼ inch) and press with a hot iron. Then fold over again and press flat again. Using your sewing machine, stitch along the hem you have made, as near to the open edge as you can. Press again.

2. Do the same to the other short edge.

3. Fold your rectangle in half lengthways, with the right sides (i.e. the patterned side) together. Match up your neat hems. Pin together. Now stitch along each short edge of your rectangle. Leave a 1 cm (⅜ inch) seam allowance on each side. Fasten off.

4. Press again. That's your lining!

1.

3.

MAKE YOUR BAG

1. Fold your rectangle of faux leather in half, with the leathery side on the inside. Pin it, and stitch up each short edge using your leather needle on the sewing machine. Again, leave a 1 cm (⅜ inch) seam allowance.

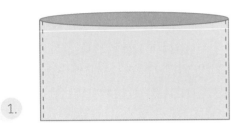

2. Turn right side out, and poke the corners out with a pencil or chopstick.

PUT THEM TOGETHER

1. Pop the cotton bag inside the leather one. Your nice patterned lining should be on display. Match up all four top edges and pin them in place. Tack them together with some bright thread and big stitches, then take out the pins.

2. Open the zip so that it falls into two pieces. Take one half and lay it along one top edge of your clutch so the right side of the zip is facing the leather side of the bag. Make sure it is the fabric part of the zip, not the teeth, which is lining up with the top edge of your clutch. Pin in place.

3. Stitch along the length of the zip, using the leather needle on your machine and a zip foot to make sure you get as close to the teeth as possible, sewing through the leather and the lining. Take out the pins.

4. Now take the other half of your zip and lay it down on the other top edge of the clutch, as you did before. Make sure the two halves match up. Pin it and sew it in place. Take out the pins.

5. Pull out the tacking.

6. You may need to hand stitch together the fabric foot end of the zip just to keep things tidy.

7. Now zip up your clutch and you're ready to go.

A SOUVENIR OF
THE CORONATION OF
H.M. QUEEN ELIZABETH II
1953

CORONATION
E II R
ELIZABETH

HIPSTER DOLLS

This cute little twosome is so cool they probably live in a converted warehouse and write a fashion blog together. They would make an ideal house-warming gift for the hipster couple in your life – or make just one as a mini boy- or girlfriend for your single pal (they may kill you though).

This project also works as an excellent stash-buster, as the dolls are made from scraps of leftover fabric and ends of yarn – and it's a good one too if you don't have a sewing machine, as it is much easier to sew the small pieces by hand.

I got a bit carried away with my dolls and would have been quite happy giving them names, knitting tiny cardigans and felting them a pet dachshund. But sometimes you just have to let go.

MATERIALS

- ✳ Black embroidery thread
- ✳ Brown yarn, about 1 ball should do it
- ✳ Dry uncooked lentils
- ✳ Matching sewing thread
- ✳ Pair of stripy socks
- ✳ Scraps of cotton and felt
- ✳ Toy stuffing
- ✳ White cotton/cotton drill, approx. 40 cm squ (16 inches squ)

EQUIPMENT

- ✳ Cotton wool
- ✳ Embroidery needle
- ✳ Fabric glue
- ✳ Iron and ironing board
- ✳ Pins
- ✳ Scissors
- ✳ Sewing machine or sewing needle
- ✳ Tracing paper and pencil
- ✳ Water soluble fabric marker pen

HOW TO MAKE A DOLL

1. Trace around the templates on p. 102. Cut out two body shapes and two arm shapes from your white cotton. Press it if it looks creased.

2. Use the template to cut out two legs from the socks. Position the template so the dark heels/toes on the sock can be used to mimic shoes on the doll's legs.

MAKING FACES

1. The first thing to do is to embroider your doll's face. Take one of the body pieces and mark out features in the face area with the fabric pen.

2. Thread your needle with two strands of brown embroidery thread and knot one end. I used back stitch to sew in the eyes, then filled in the pupils with satin stitch (see p. 13)

3. I freestyled the boy doll's beard and 'tache with more satin stitch. Remember that eyelashes, eyebrows and even the angle of the mouth will alter the dolls' expression. I was aiming for trendy insouciance – no smiles or rosy cheeks here.

4. Once you're done, weave loose ends back through your stitches on the back of the fabric and trim any stragglers. Dab off the pen with damp cotton wool.

MAKING THE BODY

1. Lay your body shape with the embroidered face in front of you, then place the second body piece on top. Pin together, and stitch all the way around the edge, leaving a 5 mm (¼ inch) seam allowance. Leave a gap on the straight bottom edge.

2. Use sharp little scissors to clip the outer curves of the body, being careful not to snip the stitching, and turn the body right side out through the gap.

3. Stuff the head and top two-thirds of the body with toy stuffing, using a pencil or chopstick to ram it in firmly.

   Fill the bottom third with the lentils – this will mean the doll can sit down without falling over.

4. Keeping the body upside down, stitch the opening closed with whip stitch (see p. 14), then fold the corners in and stitch down. The underneath of your doll will be a neat little rectangle.

ADDING THE HAIR

Hipsters would be nothing without their directional hairstyles so it's time to get creative with your leftover yarn.

FOR THE GIRL:

1. Wind your yarn around the spread-out fingers on one hand to make a double-ended loop. Once it's thick enough, about 3 cm (1⅛ inch) across, ease the circle off your hand, lay flat and cut the looped ends. Don't sneeze!

2. Place the strands in a bunch horizontally across the doll's head and back stitch (with sewing thread and needle) to the head from back to front, like a parting in the hair.

3. I plaited each side and coiled the plaits to make buns, stitching them in place. Cut a bow shape out of felt and stitch it to her head.

FOR THE BOY:

1. Wrap the yarn round his head on a slight diagonal to give him a trendy side parting. Use the sewing thread to sew it onto his head, leaving loops and curls for a rakish look.

MAKING THE LEGS

1. Fold a leg piece in half lengthways so that the right sides of the sock material (the smooth, patterned side) are on the inside, and pin. Sew together around the raw edges of the shape, leaving a tiny seam allowance. Don't sew across the top of the leg. Take out the pins and turn the leg the right way out. Now make the other leg in the same way.

2. Drop a few lentils into each leg to give the 'feet' some weight, then add stuffing almost all the way to the top. Use a pencil or chopstick again to push it in, but don't pack them as tightly as the body.

3. Back stitch straight across the top of each leg to close, tucking in raw edges.

4. Turn your doll upside down and position one leg underneath so the top of the leg matches up with the seam along the bottom of the body. The leg will be horizontal. Use whip stitch to sew the top of the leg to the body. Sew the other leg next to it.

THE ARMS

1. Like the legs, fold each arm piece in half lengthways and sew around the raw edges, leaving a tiny seam allowance. Turn each arm the right way out, drop in some lentils for the hands, then stuff.

2. Close the top of the arm by sewing at a 45 degree angle, tucking in raw edges. This means that the arms will hang down rather than stick straight out.

3. For the tattoos, thread your embroidery needle with two strands of embroidery thread, knot the end and back stitch little shapes – I chose hearts, anchors, stars and numbers for that old-school vibe.

4. Sew the arms using whip stitch onto the sides of the body, just below the neck, making sure they are angled downwards. I sewed the boy's arms onto him *after* I'd done his shirt.

ARM
(CUT 2)

BODY
(CUT 2)

LEG
(CUT 2)

TEMPLATE: ACTUAL SIZE

DRESSING THE DOLLS

This is the fun bit! Use your imagination and the scraps in your stash basket to improvise clothes – a secret bit of fabric glue here and there will make things a lot easier, as will using slightly stretchy fabric like an old T-shirt.

THE GIRL

1. For her dress, I cut a bit of leftover frill long enough to go around her body loosely. Fold over the top edge a couple of times and press with a hot iron. Fold in half widthways, with the right (patterned) sides together, and stitch up the short edge, leaving a 1cm (½ inch) seam allowance. Press the seam open.

2. Turn the dress right side out, and stitch loosely around the top (folded over) edge. Fit onto the doll and pull the thread to gather the dress. Stitch to close and add a few small stitches to secure the dress to the doll. Cut a collar shape out of felt and glue in place, adding a couple of stitches to make sure it is secure.

THE BOY

1. For the shirt, cut a rectangle out of cotton and hem each side by folding over each edge twice and stitching along. Press with a hot iron. To make the 'shirt' fit, add two darts where the armholes would be (fold a small triangle of fabric onto the wrong, non-patterned, side, press and stitch in place).

2. Fit the shirt onto the doll and stitch in place. Sew the arms over the top. Add a felt bow-tie.

Now for the dachshund . . .

FESTIVAL HEADDRESS

One of the things I love most about going to music festivals is the opportunity to let my hair down and dress up. A crazy headdress goes with any outfit and you can make one for yourself and for your music-mad friend who would rather be at Burning Man than a muddy field in Kent.

My headdress draws its inspiration from the flower garlands of pagan worshippers and burlesque stars to hippy festival-goers from the past, with probably a touch of nostalgia for my star turn as a bridesmaid in the Eighties. But, of course, you can add anything from pompoms to feathers or faux flowers, to glittery streamers or net. Just make sure you stitch it all on as tightly as possible and your headdress will last beyond this year's mud splashes to next.

MATERIALS

* 4 cm (1⅝ inch) wide black elastic, about 14 cm (5 ½ inches) long
* 4 cm (1⅝ inch) wide black grosgrain ribbon, about 50 cm (19¾ inches) long
* Matching sewing thread
* Ribbons, ribbon roses, braid
* Various colours of stretch velvet (each rose is made from a strip 10 cm x 35 cm (4 inches x 14 inches)

EQUIPMENT

* Fabric glue
* Pins
* Scissors
* Sewing machine or sewing needle

MAKING THE HEADBAND

1. Wind your ribbon around your head (or that of the person you are making the headdress for). It should go all the way round, leaving a 14 cm (5½ inch) gap at the back of the head. Trim the ribbon to size.

2. Pin each end of your elastic to the ends of the ribbon to make a loop – test it for size on your head again. It should fit snugly but not so tight you get a headache! If it is too loose, trim slices from the ribbon until it fits.

3. Take out the pins and sew the elastic to the ribbon. To do this, fold one end of the ribbon back on itself a tiny way. Tuck the end of your elastic into this, and fold it back on itself. You will have created a seam of four layers. Stitch it firmly, using zigzag stitch on your machine or with several lines of small back stitch (see p. 13) if sewing by hand.

4. Do the same at the other end of your elastic. It doesn't have to be too neat, it's for a festival, man!

MAKING THE ROSES

1. Take your strip of stretch velvet and fold in the short edges, onto the wrong side. Glue in place with the fabric glue.

2. Fold the velvet lengthways into a long strip. Glue with the fabric glue, or stitch together each short end.

3. Now thread your needle with a long strand of sewing thread and fasten it with a knot, or a few stitches in place, at one end of your strip – at the side with the raw edges – not the fold. Stitch along the length using big tacking stitches. Keep them as even as you can.

4. When you reach the other end of the strip, pull gently on the thread and push down on the velvet. The strip should gather up nicely. Arrange it in a 'rose' shape and then stitch through the base several times to hold it. You may have to tuck in any raw seams, but again don't worry about making things too neat – you've got a festival to get to!

4.

5. Make seven roses of varying colours and stitch them through their bases onto the ribbon. Start by placing the first one slightly to the right of centre and place the others either side. You may need to add a few stitches between the roses to keep them all facing the front.

DECORATE!

1. Use everything in your stash to, almost literally, chuck at your headdress. I was aiming for an English country maid/Tudor rose look, so interspersed my roses with some tiny gold ribbon roses on wire, which I wrapped around the main ribbon. I also stitched braid along the front of the ribbon and then gathered a bundle of ribbons and braid and stitched them to the back of the ribbon to one side. An upholstery tassel, meant to adorn curtains, added to the vibe. Hold a square of left-over grosgrain ribbon over the top of your bunch of ribbons (on the inside of the headdress) and sew around for extra security.

2. Add some music, noodles and sunshine and you're good to go!

FINDING RIBBONS

Always keep an eye out for ribbons! Not just on presents, ribbons can pop up round bunches of flowers, tins of fancy biscuits or chocolates, posh packaging, boxes of Christmas decorations and even cakes. While I wouldn't advocate ripping them off other people's goodies, a little judicious watching, waiting and sneaky retrieval will keep your ribbon stash full. Just don't start pulling them out of little girls' hair.

GRAND
MÈRE

whaha®
...eine Free
...Day Tea

...Decaffeinated Orthodox Teas.
...ess of Tea. No Caffeine.
...s a bright amber tea.

DOTTY ABOUT YOU QUILT

A quilt would be a truly awesome present – for someone you really, really, really like. Someone has to really give you the warm and fuzzies for you to want to stitch together lots of little squares*.

But don't worry, it doesn't have to be a drag! This little machine-made quilt is big enough to look impressive, yet you could zip through it in a weekend and be snuggling under it with someone special by Monday night.

For me, the best thing about patchwork is the excuse to delve about in those baskets of grown-up candy, i.e. fat quarters, in patchwork shops. Yes, you could very easily make this quilt using bits of stash and random cottons, but I wanted to mix and match some truly heart-felt fabrics for a kitsch cherry-pie effect.

*Conversely I once spent about 18 months hand-stitching a quilt to get over a break-up. Best. Cure. Ever. And I kept the quilt! #Win.

MATERIALS

* Backing fabric, approx. 120 cm x 160 cm (47¼ inches x 63 inches)
* Enough cotton fabric to make 165 squares, each sized 11 cm sq (4⅜ inches sq). My quilt comprised 24 pink squares, 83 red squares and 58 white squares
* Matching sewing thread
* Wadding, approx. 120 cm x 160 cm (47¼ inches x 63 inches)
* White bias binding

EQUIPMENT

* Cardboard
* Cotton wool
* Pencil
* Pins
* Ruler
* Safety pins
* Scissors
* Sewing machine
* Water soluble fabric marker pen

BEFORE YOU START

1. Before you even put scissors to fabric, work out your design. I drew several grids of 15 squares by 11 squares in my notebook and coloured in a few designs with crayons until I was happy.

2. Next, make a template. This will make your life a LOT easier. Using thin cardboard (cereal boxes are the best) measure and draw a 10 cm sq (4 inch sq) square. Then draw a 5 mm (¼ inch) border all the way around. This is the size of your seam allowance for each patchwork square. Your final template should be 11 cm (4⅜ inch) square.

3. Press all your fabric.

4. Decide on a **wrong side** of your fabric and mark out all the squares (including their hems) that you will need in each colour with your fabric pen, using the template for easy measuring. Try to mark out and cut several squares in one go to speed things up.

5. Make piles of your cut squares as you go, counting sporadically to make sure you have the right amount of each colour.

PUTTING THE QUILT TOGETHER

1. Using your diagram, lay out your squares on the floor as you want them to appear in your quilt (I am assuming you do not live in a stately home with a Knights of the Round Table-sized craft table). I used a mixture of dotty and heart-printed red cotton so this was the time to move them around within the quilt to find the most pleasing arrangement.

Take a snap of your quilt pieces, once you have laid them out, with your phone or camera. This will come in very handy, especially as you will probably have to put away your pieces at some point during the making of your quilt.

3. Place the first two squares right side (pattern side) together and pin. Stitch along the 5 mm (¼ inch) seam allowance. Take out the pin and pin on the next square. Sew along the seam allowance again. Keep going until you have a line of 15 squares.

4. Press the back of the chain, pressing open all the little seams. Put it back in place on the floor.

5. Make 11 strips as described.

6. Now sew the strips together. Pick up the first two (moving from left to right across the quilt) and place them right sides together. Pin in place. You may have to do a little manoeuvring to make sure all the squares line up. Sew all the way down along your 5 mm (¼ inch) hemline.

7. Keep going until all the strips are joined. Turn over and press open all the seams.

8. Easy peasy, you made patchwork!

BACKING THE QUILT

1. Press your backing fabric and lay it on the floor, pattern side down. Then lay the wadding on top of it. Then lay your quilt top, right side up, on top.

2. Starting in the middle of the quilt, pin all three layers together using safety pins. Use as many pins as you can, as this will stop everything slipping about.

2. Now start stitching your squares together in strips. The easiest way is to choose your first 15-square strip, running from the top to bottom of the quilt. Carefully remove them from the floor, stacking them neatly in the order they appear.

3. Now sew your quilt together. The easiest way is to stitch along all the horizontal seams and then all the vertical ones, known as 'sewing in the gutter'. This will make the lovely puffy quiltiness! Take out the safety pins.

FINISHING THE QUILT

1. Trim your backing fabric and wadding to the size of the patchwork top. Try to keep the edges as straight as you can.

2. Open out one side of your bias binding and, starting at one corner of the quilt, lay it all along one side, with right sides together, placing the open edge of the bias binding along the edge of your quilt. Pin as you go.

3. Sew all the way along the fold line of the bias binding.

4. Now fold the bias binding over the top of the raw edge of your quilt and pin in place on the other side. Whip stitch (see p. 14) it in place. Press.

5. Do the same along each side of the quilt, folding each corner neatly and tucking in the raw edges.

6. Remove the pins and you're done!

QUILTING BY HAND

You don't have to be a complete masochist to sew a quilt by hand – but it helps! I'm joking – a handmade quilt is very satisfying to make and – I think – looks a lot nicer and produces a softer, more personal result.

Make two cardboard templates – one 11 cm sq (4 ⅜ inches sq), one 10 cm sq (4 inches sq). Use the smaller template to cut out 165 squares from paper. Use the other template to cut out your fabric squares as required.

Pin all the paper templates onto the wrong side of the fabric squares, making sure they are in the middle. With each square, trim off the four excess corners, fold each hem onto the wrong side of the square, press with a hot iron, and tack in place.

Once you have finished every square, join them in strips as before, joining them together with small whip stitches. Join all the strips together.

Turn your patchwork over, snip all the tacking and pull it out. Then rip out all the paper. If I am using old newspaper, I like to leave a square or two in place to date my quilt for posterity's sake.

Press your patchwork and construct the quilt as before.

BLOOMING LOVELY

Forget lycra – the only way to be seen cycling is with these saucy underdrawers peeking out from your flying skirts. Or show them off over some tights.

I was inspired to make these rather gothic beauties after one too many commutes to work when I would need three hands – two for the bike handlebars and one to hold my skirt down to stop me flashing my unmentionables at the rest of the traffic. These bloomers are easy to make and comfortable to wear, while the fluorescent ribbon adds a nice safety-conscious touch for those cycling on a dim day.

Make a pair for the Pashley princess in your life – or knock up a pair in soft brushed cotton as cute PJ bottoms.

MATERIALS

- ⁂ Broderie anglais, 1 m (39⅜ inches)
- ⁂ Fluorescent ribbon, 1 m (39⅜ inches)
- ⁂ Patterned fabric – polyester or cotton/polyester mix, 1 m (39⅜ inches)
- ⁂ 2.5 cm (1 inch) wide elastic, 1 m (39⅜ inches)
- ⁂ Matching sewing thread

EQUIPMENT

- ⁂ Iron and ironing board
- ⁂ Photocopier
- ⁂ Pins
- ⁂ Safety pin
- ⁂ Scissors
- ⁂ Sewing machine

WHAT TO DO

1. Photocopy the templates from p. 120, increasing by 400 per cent. These create a UK size 12 (US size 8). To make them larger, add about 2 cm (⅝ inch) around all the edges, per dress size. Likewise, to make them smaller, reduce the pattern by 2 cm (⅝ inch) around all the edges, per dress size. Once you have the righhtsize add a 1.5 cm (⅝ inch) seam allowance all the way around.

2. Press your fabric. Fold in half, placing the selvedges (sealed edges) together. Place the front and back patterns on the material. Cut out two front pieces and two back pieces from the templates. Make sure the templates lie along the straight grain of the fabric.

3. Place the front right leg piece and the back right leg piece together, right sides facing. Pin in place. Stitch together along the inner leg leaving a 1.5 cm (⅝ inch) seam allowance. Turn your sewing machine to zigzag stitch and sew all along the raw edge of the fabric. This will help reduce fraying.

4. Place the front left leg piece and the back left leg piece together, right sides facing. Pin in place. Stitch together along the inner leg seam leaving a 1.5 cm (⅝ inch) seam allowance. Turn your sewing machine to zigzag stitch and sew all along the raw edge of the fabric.

5. Match up the centre front seams on the right and left legs right sides together and pin in place. Stitch all the way down and back up the other side, joining the centre back seams and leaving a 1.5 cm (⅝ inch) seam allowance. As before, zigzag along the raw edges. Take out the pins.

6. With the right sides together, pin the side seams and sew along, leaving a 1.5 cm (⅝ inch) seam allowance. Zigzag the edges. Take out the pins.

7. Press all the seams open with a hot iron. Now your project should resemble some bloomers!

GETTING WAISTED

1. Now you need to make the casing for your elastic around the waistband. With the bloomers still inside out, fold down the top upper edge of the garment by 5 mm (¼ inch) and press. Then turn over the top of the garment again 3 cm (1¼ inches). Press in place, then pin.

2. Now sew all along this seam with a straight stitch, leaving a small gap to pass the elastic through. Take out the pins.

3. Measure the length of elastic you want. The easiest way is to take the desired waist measurement and add 2.5 cm (1 inch). Cut.

4. Hook the safety pin into the end of your elastic (don't forget to close the pin!). Use the safety pin to thread your elastic through the hole in the casing, all the way round the waistband and out the other side. Use the safety pin to hold the two ends together in a circle.

5. Turn your bloomers the right way round and try them on, or try them on your cyclist pal. Now's the time to adjust the elastic to fit. Once you're happy, take them off again and turn inside out.

6. Stitch across the elastic several times in the correct place. Take out the safety pin and trim any excess elastic. Let it pop back inside the casing and sew up the hole.

THE TRUE STORY

Bloomers were named after Amelia Bloomer, the fashion-forward American women's rights campaigner who championed the wearing of these 'bifurcated' garments in the 1850s as part of the drive for more rational dress for women. They didn't really catch on as outerwear until the late 19th century, when more women began to bicycle — even so, the combination of bloomers and bikes continued to shock, with fears that this conspicuous behaviour could lead to greater immorality and more masculine behaviour.

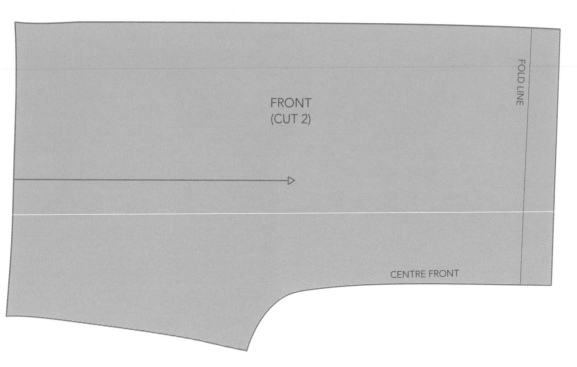

FRONT
(CUT 2)

FOLD LINE

CENTRE FRONT

INCREASE BY 400% FOR A UK SIZE 12 (US SIZE 8)

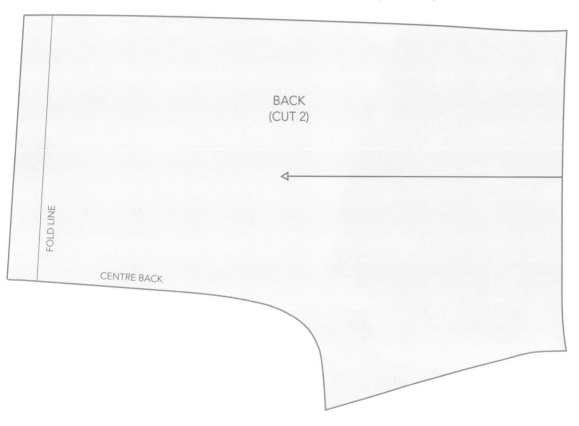

BACK
(CUT 2)

FOLD LINE

CENTRE BACK

GET SHORTY

1. Now it's time to finish the legs. Turn the bloomers inside out. Turn one bottom hem 5 mm (¼ inch) onto the wrong side and press. Then turn over the hem again 1 cm (⅜ inch) and press. Stitch all the way around the leg along the edge of the seam. Press.

2. Repeat on the other leg.

3. Now turn your bloomers right way out.

4. Place your broderie anglais or eyelet lace all the way around the bottom edge of one leg – you will want the top edge about 1.5 cm (⅝ inch) from the bottom of the leg. Overlap the two ends of lace by about 1.5 cm (⅝ inch), folding under the raw edge of the top piece. Pin in place.

5. Stitch the lace to the leg, following a line just above the eyelet holes.

6. Repeat on the other leg.

7. Cut your fluorescent ribbon into two 50 cm (19 ¾ inch) lengths. Thread one through the holes in the eyelet lace on one leg, beginning on the outer side of the leg. Pull the lengths equal, gathering the material, and tie in a bow. Trim 'v' shapes into the ends of the ribbon to prevent fraying.

8. Repeat on the other leg. Happy cycling!

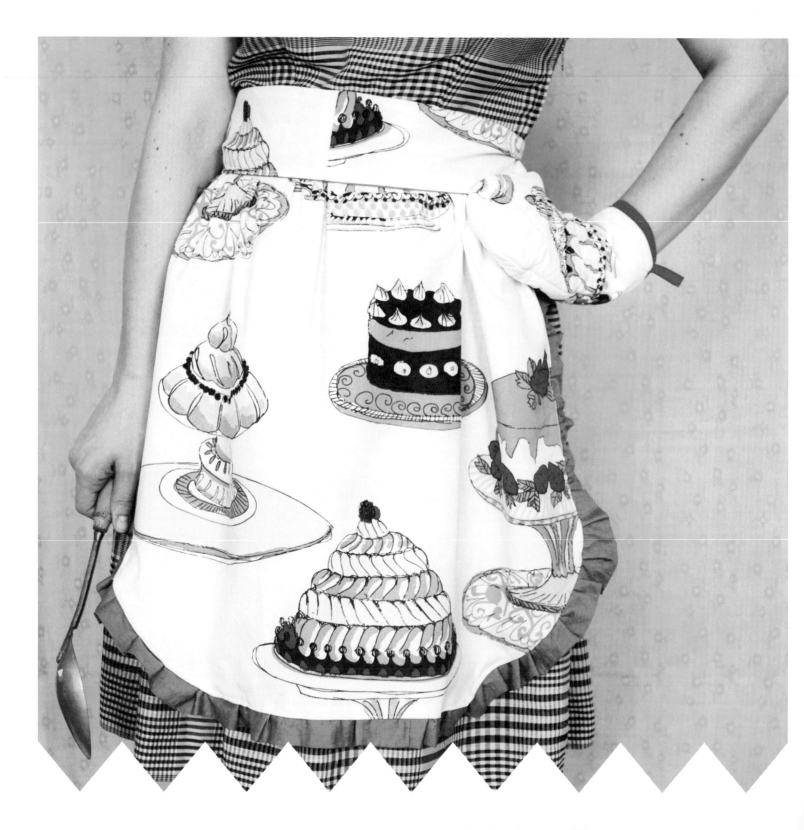

GOT IT COVERED

This sassy, frilly apron will zing up the drabbest kitchen or the dullest meal – oh and protect your clothes from splashes and spills.

My pattern is also super versatile. Ditch the frills for a plainer style, or go to the other extreme and add even more frills in rainbow layers for an über-girly look. Whip up a pocket (see p. 127) for the cooks who are always losing their recipes.

A tough cotton fabric works best – I was lucky to find my cake-patterned remnants in a bargain bin. I think they were offcuts of curtain material – I would love to see the crazy house those ended up in!

MATERIALS

* Matching sewing thread
* Patterned cotton, 60 cm x 50 cm (23⅝ inches x 19¾ inches) for the apron plus 2 m x 10 cm (78½ inches x 4 inches) for the apron ties
* Plain cotton, 2 m x 10 cm (78½ inches x 4 inches) for the apron ties plus 8 cm x 2.6 m (3⅛ inches x 102 inches) for the frill

EQUIPMENT

* Iron and ironing board
* Pinking shears
* Pins
* Scissors

HOW TO MAKE THE APRON

1. Grab your apron piece and give it a good press. Place in front of you so the longer sides are running horizontally. Fold in half sideways and pin. Trim off the bottom right hand corner in a curve – you can mark it off with a fabric pen first or just go for it with the scissors.

2. Take out the pins and open the apron up; you should have a symmetrical square-ish 'u' shape.

3. Using pinking shears, trim around the shape of your apron to prevent fraying. Fold over the pinked edge about 1 cm (⅜ inch) onto the wrong (i.e. plain) side of the apron all the way around the curved edge (not the top straight edge) and press. Snip the curves to make it easier to fold. Don't worry, this will be covered up.

4. Fold over the top straight edge of your apron onto the wrong side 1 cm (⅜ inch) and press, then fold over again 1 cm (⅜ inch), and press. Stitch along the open edge of the fold.

HOW TO MAKE THE FRILL

1. The frill is basically a long strip, about twice as long as the curved edges of your apron.

   You may need to join two strips together to make a long enough frill. To do so, cut two strips, 8 cm (3⅛ inches) wide, from your plain fabric and place one on top of the other, matching two short ends. Sew straight across leaving a 1 cm (⅜ in) hem. Press open. When you ruffle up your frill you will be able to hide the seam.

2. Fold your strip in half lengthways, with the 'right' sides on the inside and any seams on the outside. Press flat. Pin.

3. Sew along one short edge and all the way down the long open edge, leaving a 5 mm (¼ in) seam allowance. Fasten off.

4. Turn your tube round the right way through the gap left at one end, and press flat. Press in a small hem at the open end of the strip, and sew across using straight stitch on your sewing machine or by hand using a whip stitch (see p. 14) for extra neatness.

5. Press again for good measure.

6. Now thread your needle with a long piece of sewing thread in a contrast colour and knot one end. Starting at one end of the strip, on the side with the seam, tack all the way along to the other end with large, but neat stitches.

7. When you reach the other end, carefully pull on the thread to gather the strip into a gentle frill. It is easier to gather in stages – gather a section tautly, then distribute the gathers by hand before moving onto the next stage.

8. Once the whole strip is frilled, sew over and over in place to fasten off.

9. Now attach the frill to the apron. Turn the apron over so that the back is facing upwards. Arrange your frill all the way around the outer edge – pinning as you go – with the neat folded edge facing outwards, leaving about 1 cm (⅜ in) on the wrong side of the apron. You may have to create some of your own folds in the frill to make sure it fits the apron curves neatly.

10. Stitch the frill in place using a straight stitch on your machine, pulling out the pins as you go. Pull out the gathering stitch too.

MAKING THE APRON TIES

1. The apron ties are made in a similar way to the frill – as before you may have to join two strips of fabric to make long enough pieces.

2. Place the patterned apron tie piece, and the plain piece, together, right sides facing. Pin.

3. Sew along one long side, one short edge, and back up the other long edge, leaving a 5 mm (¼ inch) seam allowance. Fasten off securely.

4. Turn your tube the right way around through the open end. Press flat, and tuck in the raw edges of the remaining open side.

5. Stitch straight across, or use whip stitch to close. Press.

FINISHING OFF

1. Thread your needle with contrasting thread again and knot one end. Beginning on one side of the top straight hem of your apron, tack across with large, neat stitches. When you reach the other side, pull gently until gathers form across your apron top.

2. Arrange them neatly (you don't want one side of your apron puffier than the other!). When you're happy with it, fasten off.

3. Now fold your apron tie strip in half to find the centre and stick a pin in to mark the place. Fold your apron in half too and do the same. Now match up the pins, placing your strip right side out on the front of the apron. It will cover up the bulky folds at the top of your apron. Pin in place.

4. Now sew straight across the bottom edge of your strip. Do it twice for extra strength. Take out the pins.

5. Trim any trailing threads and press your apron.

6. Now sling it round your waist and tie with a big fancy bow. If you're giving it to someone else, take it off now – but I bet you won't want to!

POCKETING THE GOODS

The easiest way to make a big ol' pocket for your apron is to cut a 27 cm x 17 cm (10⅝ inches x 6¾ inches) rectangle of your patterned fabric (or even go properly 'migraine' and use a clashing print). Lay it right (patterned) side down and fold in one side 5 mm (¼ inch) and press. Fold over another 5 mm (¼ inch) and press again. Do the same on each side of the rectangle. Sew along the four seams. Press again.

Fold the piece in half, short sides together, and press a crease. Open out again.

Before you gather your apron (see Finishing Off opposite), position the big pocket where you want it to go and pin in place. Using either white sewing thread, or a bright contrast colour, sew down one short side and along the bottom edge until you reach your pressed crease. Stitch up this line – when you reach the top, leave the needle in, lift your machine foot and rotate the material 180 degrees. Then put the machine foot down and sew back down the way you came, complete the bottom edge of the pocket and sew up the other short side. Finish off.

JUST GLOVELY

If you're anything like me, the moment my pastry reaches that optimum golden brown or my muffins achieve the perfect fluff, or, more likely, the fire alarm goes off, the first thing I grab is an old tea towel to get the hot stuff out the oven.

But no more! This snug glove is the perfect gift for kitchen maestros – pair it with the apron on p. 122 and a pretty cake tin and you're practically inviting a homemade cake in gratitude. See, it's all give, give, give with us.

MATERIALS

* Matching sewing thread
* Plain cotton, 30 cm x 60 cm (12 inches x 23⅝ inches)
* Tough, patterned cotton, 30 cm x 60 cm (12 inches x 23 ⅝ inches)
* Wadding, 30 cm x 60 cm (12 inches x 23⅝ inches)

EQUIPMENT

* Cotton wool
* Iron and ironing board
* Newspaper or tracing paper
* Pencil
* Pins
* Ruler
* Scissors
* Sewing machine
* Water soluble fabric pen

WHAT TO DO

1. First, make your pattern. Use newspaper or tracing paper and draw a glove shape around one hand, keeping the fingers slightly spread. The pattern will extend to just below your wrist and about 2.5 cm (1 inch) wider than the dimensions of your hand.

2. Use the pattern to cut two from the patterned fabric (remember to do one facing to the right, one facing to the left!). Cut two from the lining fabric and four from the wadding.

3. You are going to make two halves of the glove then stitch them together. To make one half, sandwich together a patterned glove piece (pattern side down), two wadding pieces, then a plain piece. Pin together.

4. Using fabric pen and a ruler, mark out diagonal lines across the plain side of the glove, about 3 cm (1⅛ inches) apart. Turn the glove and mark out diagonal lines going the other way.

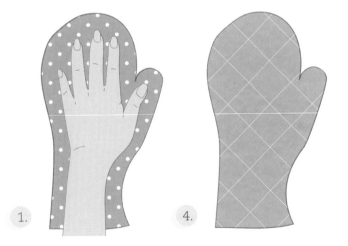

1.   4.

5. Using the sewing machine (you can hand stitch, but the sewing machine results will be a lot quicker and neater), sew along the lines you have marked out. This will give your glove a lovely quilted effect. Take out pins.

6. Do the same to make the other side of the glove – don't forget to reverse it! You need one right hand and one left hand. Use damp cotton wool to dab off the fabric pen marks.

7. Now make the strip to seal the bottom of the glove. Cut two strips of the lining fabric, each 15 cm x 4 cm (6 inches x 1⅝ inches). Fold in half lengthways and press. Open out, and fold the long raw edges into the inner fold line you have made. Press. Fold in half down the original fold line again and press.

8. Take one strip, fold it around the bottom edge of one glove half and pin in place. Sew down the top side of your strip using matching sewing thread – make sure you are sewing down the top edge of the other side of the strip at the same time. Trim any excess. Now add the strip to the other glove piece.

9. Now make the little hanging loop. Cut a piece of your lining fabric, about 4 cm x 10 cm (1⅝ inches x 4 inches). Fold it in half lengthways and press. As before, fold in the two long edges into the middle fold line, press. Fold in half again, and press. Sew down the long open edge of the strip in matching thread and press. You should have a tough little rectangular strip.

10. Place your two glove pieces on top of each other, so that the patterned sides are on the inside and the thumb shapes are lined up. Fold your little strip in half and tuck it in between the two pieces, so that the raw ends line up with the raw edges of the glove pieces on the 'finger' side of the shape. Pin in place.

11. Sew around the outer edges of the glove shape, leaving as small a hem as you can. Trim any excess.

12. Turn the glove the right way round and poke the shape out with a pencil or chopstick. Your hanging loop should be on the outside now. Press flat.

GET SPORTY

At school we had to make our own drawstring bags, embroidered with our initials, to keep our gym kit in. By the end of term there was always at least one pair of socks or swimming hat that had been festering in its depths for the past 12 weeks – and I have been wary of 'gym bags' – and in fact anything involving sticks, balls and a field – ever since.

Luckily this bag is light, airy and, I like to think, a stylish present for your favourite yoga fanatic or gym bunny. No sweaty netball skirts in sight.

See if you can find a polyester mesh fabric to make your bag – I was lucky enough to chance upon a giant 'Fresh Prince of Bel Air'-style basketball vest in a charity shop which was perfect.

MATERIALS

* Black cotton fabric, 1 m (39⅜ inches)
* Black zip (closed-end), 40 cm (15¾ inches) in length
* Cotton webbing tape, 2 m (78¾ inches)
* Matching sewing thread
* Polyester mesh fabric, 1 m (39⅜ inches)

EQUIPMENT

* Compass
* Dressmaker's chalk
* Iron and ironing board
* Newspaper
* Pencil or a chopstick
* Pins
* Scissors
* Sewing machine
* Sewing needle

WHAT TO DO

First of all make the main piece of your bag.

1. Cut a 71 cm x 51 cm (28 inches x 20 inches) rectangle from the polyester fabric and the same from the black cotton. Place right sides together and pin.

2. Stitch all the way around the four sides, leaving a 1.5 cm (⅝ inch) seam allowance. Leave a small gap. Remove all the pins and turn your rectangle the right way out through the gap. Poke the corners out using something long and pointy like a pencil or a chopstick.

3. Tuck in the raw edges where you left the gap, and sew the opening closed. Press your rectangle on the cotton side.

THE ENDS

1. Use some newspaper to make a circle template for the ends of your bag. Use a compass to draw a 22 cm (8 ⅝ inch) diameter circle on the paper and cut out.

2. Use the template to cut two circles from the polyester mesh and two from the black cotton.

3. Place one polyester mesh circle and one black cotton circle right sides together. Pin. Stitch all the way around the circumference, leaving a 1 cm (⅜ inch) seam allowance. As before, leave a small gap. Turn your circle the right side out through the gap and poke into shape with your chopstick.

4. Tuck in the raw edges of the gap and sew in place. Press flat on the cotton side.

5. Repeat for the other circle.

ASSEMBLING THE BAG

1. Grab your rectangular piece and fold it in half, short edges together, right sides facing. Use some dressmaker's chalk to mark the fold. Now mark the quarter points and the eighth points Open out again.

2. Fold your circles in half, right sides facing and, in the same way, mark it into eight segments. Open out.

3. Hold one of the circle pieces vertically against a short edge of the rectangle (with the right sides facing) matching up the chalk marks. Using a lot of pins, pin the straight edge to the circumference of your circle piece starting with your chalk marks so the pieces are evenly divided. You may have to pleat it in places to make sure it fits – but don't worry, this will make your bag look nice and squashy.

4. Once you have finished, repeat on the other end of the bag. Using a needle and cotton tack firmly in place. Remove pin and sew in place by hand or with your sewing machine. Turn the bag the right way out. Now you should have a tube shape.

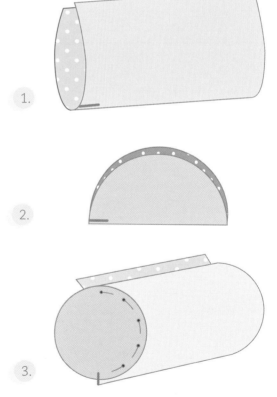

1.

2.

3.

FINISHING OFF

1. Now you need to insert the zip. Hold it along the length of your bag opening. It will be a little shorter than your bag, so work out the excess and stitch the bag opening closed at each end to make sure your zip will fit snugly.

2. Now open the zip a short way and place one half (zip side up) along one side of your bag opening on the INSIDE of the bag. Pin in place. Make sure the bag fabric covers the ends of your zip but does not impede it.

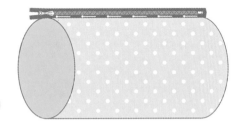

2.

3. Using a zipper foot on your machine, stitch along the length of your zip, taking out the pins as you go.

4. Now pin the other half of the zip to the other side of your bag opening, on the INSIDE of the bag. As before, stitch together, removing the pins.

5. Zip your bag closed and check it works.

ADDING THE STRAPS

1. Open your bag and stuff it lightly with an old towel or similar to bulk it up – this will help you add your straps. Zip closed again.

2. Pin one end of your cotton webbing tape to the underside of your bag, about 12 cm (4¾ inches) from the outer seam. Place it around the bag to the top edge, pinning as you go. After adding a loop long enough to hook over a shoulder, start pinning the strap to the bag again, about 12 cm (4¾ inches) from the outer seam.

3. Continue pinning your strap, until it meets where it started. Cut the tape. Fold the end under and pin on top of the beginning of the tape.

3.

4. Repeat for the other strap.

5. Open the zip and take out the stuffing. Now stitch your handle in place using the machine. Starting about 6 cm (2⅜ inches) down from the zip, stitch a square shape on the tape for extra hold. Now stitch along the outside edge of the tape, following it until you reach the same position 6 cm (2⅜ inches) down from the zip on the other side of the bag. Stitch another square and stitch back down the other side of your strap until you reach he beginning again. Finish off.

6. Repeat on the other strap.

4.
it's a
wrap

NICE TO GREET YOU

Decorating cards doesn't have to be hard or time-consuming. These designs are easy-peasy and can be adapted to suit any occasion.

I use ready-made blank cards and envelopes (you can buy multipacks for about the same price as one shop-bought birthday card). Cards are the easiest – and the quickest – way to make a gift really personal, so get out the sequins!

CHRISTMAS TREE

This wee Christmas tree reminds me of primary school art classes towards the end of the autumn term, when pretty much everything we made was some kind of glitter-bedecked 'present' for lucky relatives.

I'd like to pretend this card is more sophisticated, but it's not really; just try not to glue anything to your face like you did when you were eight.

MATERIALS

- Card and envelope
- Cup sequins/star-shaped flat sequin/ large round sequin or pailette
- Royal blue felt scraps
- Sewing thread

EQUIPMENT

- PVA glue
- Scissors

WHAT TO DO

1. Make the tree by cutting out five isosceles triangles diminishing in size. Beginning with the largest triangle at the bottom, layer the four smaller triangles on top in order of size, arranging them into a fir tree shape. Glue together.

2. Starting at the top of your tree, stitch on your baubles (cup sequins) with one stitch per sequin.

3. To make the pot, snip the sides off a large round sequin or pailette.

4. Place your tree on the front of your card, and position the star-shaped sequin under the point, and the pot-shaped sequin in the middle under the tree. Glue the sequins to the card. Then glue your tree in place on top.

ENVELOPE

I decorated the matching envelope by stitching a line of sequins along the top right edge.

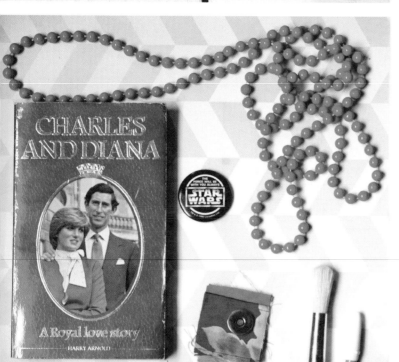

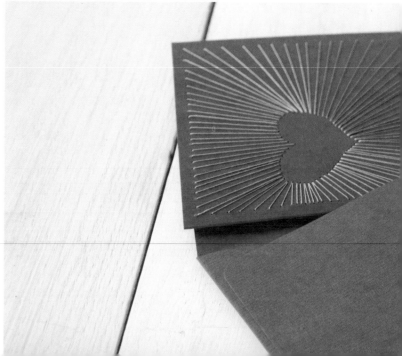

HEART-BURST

This card is super-simple to make but looks really effective. It would work as a really special birthday card – you could even add some seed beads or sequins onto the threads for extra glam.

MATERIALS

* Blue card and envelope
* Sewing thread in grey or silver

EQUIPMENT

* Needle
* Pencil
* Ruler
* Scissors

WHAT TO DO

1. First off, draw a border on the front of your card 5 mm (¼ inch) from the edge using a ruler and light pencil marks. This will keep your lines straight.

2. Sketch out a small heart shape on the front of your card.

3. Thread a long length of silver or grey sewing thread onto your needle and knot the end. Starting in the top left-hand corner of the box you drew, make a long stitch ending on the outline of your heart. Make a tiny sideways stitch on the back of your card. Your next stitch will go from the heart outline back to the border of the card.

3.

4. Continue all the way round. The lines will all converge on the heart outline – you may have to reuse the same holes.

5. Keep the back of the card tidy by weaving excess threads through old stitches.

6. Decorate the envelope by using stitches to mark out a heart shape on the top left of the envelope. Be careful not to tear the paper.

WHIRLY-GIRL

This perky little card will get your recipient in a spin. One for a birthday girl or boy.

MATERIALS

* Card and envelope
* Red button
* Sewing thread
* Stamp and ink
* Stickers
* White paper

EQUIPMENT

* Pencil
* Ruler
* Sewing needle
* Scissors

WHAT TO DO

1. First decorate your card. Affix two rows of stickers to the top and bottom of the card.

2. Now make your windmill. Cut a piece of paper 13 cm (5⅛ inches) square. If you have a stamp and ink, print your design over one side. Alternatively, you could cut a square of wrapping paper or other pretty paper to the same size and glue it to the back of your white square.

3. With the patterned side of the paper facing up, find the centre of your square and dot with the pencil. Using the ruler, mark four lines coming in from each corner towards the middle, stopping about 1 cm (⅜ inch) from the centre. Cut along these lines – your square will now be marked into four triangles.

4. Place your square at an angle before you. Fold the top corner of one triangle towards you, so the point meets the centre of your square. Gently compress the paper to make a gentle fold. Glue the point in place.

4.

5. Revolve the square and fold down the next corner. Keep going until all four points are glued into the centre.

6. Now place your windmill into the centre of your card. Using red sewing thread, stitch the windmill in place through its centre, at the same time passing through the holes of the button. You should be able to turn the windmill.

7. Cover up your stitches on the back of the card with a sticker.

8. Decorate the envelope with a small rectangle of white paper – if you have a stamp, decorate it, or just leave it plain. Glue in place, then decorate the edges with a row of overlapping stickers.

FOR THE WIN

Who doesn't want to feel like a winner? This detachable rosette makes an extra little present.

MATERIALS

* Badge pin
* Card
* Felt
* Ribbon, 15 cm (6 inches) long
* Sewing thread
* Strip of fabric, 20 cm x 6 cm (8 in x 2⅜ inches)
* Washi tape

EQUIPMENT

* Iron and ironing board
* PVA Glue
* Scissors
* Sewing needle

MAKING THE ROSETTE

1. Fold the short ends of your fabric strip onto the wrong (non-patterned) side and press. Fix in place with glue.

2. Fold your strip in half lengthways and press.

3. Knot the end of your thread and run a line of stitches along the long raw edge of your folded strip. When you reach the end, pull gently, pushing on the fabric, to create pleats.

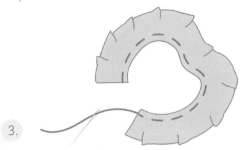

3.

4. Curl your fabric in a circle and stitch through the centre. Overlap one end of the strip over the other and sew together.

5. Cut two 'ribbons' from the felt. Cut two circle shapes from the felt, one about 4 cm (1⅝ inches) in diameter, one about 5 cm (2 inches) in diameter. Position the 'ribbons' on the back of the gathered circle and stitch in place. Cover with the larger circle and stitch in place, sewing around the circumference of the circle.

6. Turn over and stitch the smaller circle to the front of the rosette, sewing around the circumference of the circle.

7. Glue the badge pin to the larger circle on the back of the rosette and stitch in place.

FINISHING THE CARD

1. Cut a slit at the top and bottom of your card and thread the ribbon through. Glue the ends onto the back of the card. Cut two rectangles of card and glue in place to cover the raw ends.

2. Pin your rosette to the ribbon.

3. Decorate the envelope with strips of paper and washi tape in matching colours.

WRAP STARS

I'm as seduced as the next person by the glittering array of wrapping paper in the shops, not to mention the tags and bows and ribbons and gift tags, but it also feels sad (and wasteful) to chuck it all away once the presents are opened.

These pretty boxes and bags will hopefully be reused every now and again by their recipients – plus the Japanese-style wrapping cloths are a present in themselves.

DRAWSTRING BAG

This sweet little bag is perfect for awkwardly shaped presents – so adapt the pattern to make it as big or small as you like.

MATERIALS

* Matching sewing thread
* Ribbon
* Stripy cotton fabric, 34 cm x 40 cm (13⅛ inches x 15 ¾ in)

EQUIPMENT

* Iron and ironing board
* Safety pin
* Scissors
* Sewing machine

WHAT TO DO

1. Press your fabric.

2. Fold over the top edge a tiny way onto the wrong (non-patterned) side, press, and then fold over another 1 cm (⅜ inches). Press. Sew along the folded edge, either using a straight stitch on your machine or whip stitch (see p. 14) if sewing by hand. Press.

3. Fold the fabric in half width-ways, right sides together. Pin.

4. Stitch along the bottom edge and up the open side, leaving a 1 cm (⅜ inch) seam allowance. Finish off. Take out the pins and press.

5. Turn the bag the right way round and press again.

6. To make the channel for your ribbon, fold the top of your bag over, right sides together. The fold line needs to be 7.5 cm (3 inches) from the top of your bag. Press.

7. Fold the material back on itself (like a zigzag) and pin in place. You should be making a 2.5 cm (1 inch) wide channel around the bag, with an extra 2.5 cm (1 inch) top edge of the fabric remaining. Press.

8. Stitch along the bottom edge of your fold, all the way round the bag, and then again around the top of the channel.

9. Cut a small opening in the channel at the front of the bag. If you like, fold the edges of the hole back and hem.

10. Put the safety pin through the end of your ribbon, close it and push through the hole. Thread all the way round the channel and back out the opening. Remove the safety pin and trim v-shapes into the ends of the ribbon to prevent fraying. Pull tight and tie in a bow.

SQUARE POUCH

This cute little box is perfect for a tiny sparkly present –
don't forget the tissue paper!

MATERIALS

* Three strands of ribbon
* Washi tape
* White card

EQUIPMENT

* Hole punch
* Pencil
* Ruler
* Scissors

WHAT TO DO

1. Cut a strip of white card 10 cm (4 inches) wide 24 cm
   (9 ½ inches) long. Draw lines across 10 cm (4 in) from each
   end. Score lightly with your open scissors blade against
   the ruler. Use the hole punch to make a hole in the centre
   of each short end.

2. Cut two triangles from the remainder of your white
   card, 4 cm (1⅝ inches) across the base and 10 cm
   (4 inches) high.

3. Place one triangle at the centre of the side of the strip of
   card, and fold the strip up around to fit against the
   triangle-sides. Stick together with washi tape.

4. Fit the other triangle into the other end of the little box
   and fix with washi tape. Now add washi tape along the
   bottom four edges of the box.

5. Thread the three long ribbons through the holes made
   by the hole punch and tie in a bow.

BROWN PAPER LETTER BAG

I often wrap my Christmas presents in brown paper – tougher and more reusable than tacky wrapping paper, plus it looks smart with ribbons or yarn wrapped around your present. This little bag is perfect for what my brother always used to disdainfully call 'squidgy' presents, plus the stencilled letter adds an extra personal touch.

MATERIALS

* Brown paper
* Newspaper
* Washi tape
* White/blue card
* White paint

EQUIPMENT

* Glue
* Hole punch
* Pencil
* Ruler
* Scissors
* Stubby brush or sponge

WHAT TO DO

1. Cut a piece of brown paper 27 cm x 48.5 cm (10⅝ inches x 19⅛ inches)

2. Draw a line along one long edge, 5 cm (2 inches) from the bottom. Then mark out vertical lines at 2.5 cm (1 inch), at 5 cm (2 inches) further on, again after 18 cm (7 inches) and finally after another 5 cm (2 inches).

3. Cut up from the bottom edge of the paper along each vertical line until you meet the horizontal line.

DECORATE THE BAG

1. To make your stencil, sketch out a letter template onto newspaper and cut out. Place it on one of the large rectangles marked out on your brown paper. Dip your brush or sponge into white paint and dab lightly around the edges of your stencil.

2. Carefully remove the stencil and you should have the silhouette of your letter marked out on the paper.

3. While it is drying, use the hole punch to cut out a pile of circles from your white and blue card. Glue them in place around the letter, using white nearer to the letter and blue as you move away.

FINISHING THE BAG

1. Complete the bag by folding along each of the vertical lines. The edge of the 2.5 cm (1 inch) strip folds inside the fourth side of your bag. Glue in place.

2. Fold up the short flaps of the bottom of the bag. Fold one long flap under and glue to the short flaps. Fold the second long flap under and glue in place.

3. Reinforce the edges of the bag with washi tape.

4. Cut two 1.5 cm (⅝ inch) wide strips from brown paper as the handles and glue in place at the top of the bag, on the inside. Add a strip of washi tape to decorate.

WHITE CARD BAG

This lovely bag will make any present look inviting. Make it in the same way as the brown paper bag.

MATERIALS

* Silver ribbon
* Washi tape
* White card

EQUIPMENT

* Craft knife
* Cutting mat
* Pencil
* PVA glue
* Ruler
* Scissors

1. Make this bag in the same way as the brown paper bag opposite. Trim with washi tape along the long edges and undersides, and around the top.

2. To make the handles, use the craft knife to cut four slits in the top of the bag, each an equal distance from the top and the sides, and about 1.5 cm (⅝ inches) wide. Cut two pieces of silver ribbon. Thread the ends of one through each slit on one side of the bag, so the ends of the ribbon are on the outside. Knot each end and cut into a V. Repeat to make the other handle.

WRAPPING CLOTHS

The traditional Japanese way of wrapping presents is called *furoshiki*. Once used to carry clothes to the public baths, these gorgeous cloths are today made out of all sorts of fabric from silk to cotton and are used to wrap lunch boxes (bento) as well as making a beautiful and reusable wrap for presents.

Of course you can use any fabric to wrap your present, but here are two ways to decorate cotton for an extra handmade touch.

First cut a square of white cotton large enough to loosely go around your present. Fold the edges in twice into the smallest hem you can, stitch around, and press. If you are feeling lazy, simply trim the edges with pinking shears.

SQUARES

Remember making potato prints at school? This is just a grown-up version. I love the slightly wavy design made by the natural textures.

1. Cut a leftover raw potato (or squash or similar fleshy vegetable) into a chunk about 2.5 cm sq (1 inch sq).

2. Brush blue fabric paint onto your potato square and stamp your fabric in a chequerboard-effect.

3. Once you've finished, make sure it's dry then press with a hot iron to seal the fabric paint.

TRIANGLES

This layered effect is made using masking tape and creates a slightly crazy 1980s effect.

1. Use narrow masking tape to mark out dozens of different-sized triangles on your fabric.

2. Pour a blob or two of fabric paint into an old bowl with a splash of water to mix. Using a brush or sponge, fill in all your triangle shapes. Allow to dry.

3. Remove the masking tape and, reusing it where you can, mark out a load more triangles, overlapping the first ones.

4. Add another splash or two of water to your fabric paint to create a paler colour, mix it up, and fill in all the new triangles. Allow to dry.

5. Now mark out your final set of triangles with the masking tape. This time use the fabric paint straight from the jar for full colour.

6. Once it's dry, remove all the masking tape and press to set the colour.

HOW TO WRAP

The easiest way to wrap a present *furoshiki* style is to place it in the centre of your square, on the diagonal. Fold one corner of the fabric in, tucking it around your present if necessary. Repeat on the opposite corner. Now draw in the remaining two corners and tie in a loose double-knot.

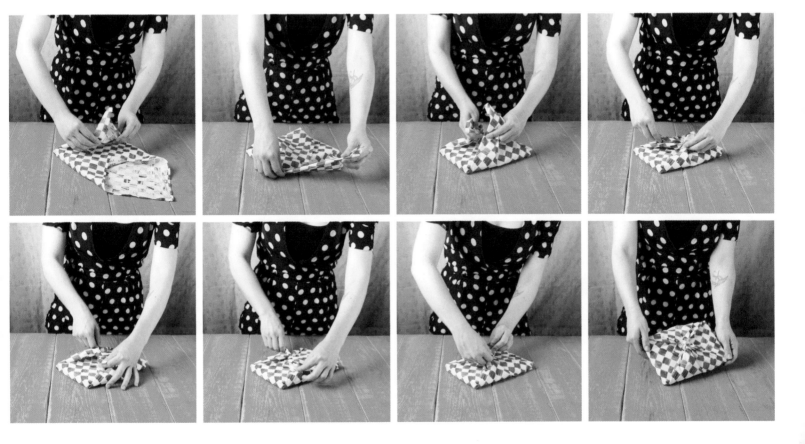

STOCKISTS

UK

BEDECKED FINE TRIMMINGS
5 Castle Street
Hay-on-Wye HR3 5DF
Tel: 01497 822 769
www.bedecked.co.uk

BEYOND FABRICS
67 Columbia Road
London E2 7RG
Tel: 0207 729 5449
www.beyond-fabrics.co.uk

CLOTH HOUSE
47/98 Berwick Street
London W1F 8SJ
Tel: 0207 7437 5155/0207 7287 1555
www.clothhouse.com

THE ETERNAL MAKER
41 Terminus Road
Chichester
West Sussex PO19 8TX
Tel: 01243 788174
www.eternalmaker.com

KLEINS
5 Noel Street
London W1F 8GD
Tel: 0207 437 6162
www.kleins.co.uk

MANDORS FABRIC STORE
Glasgow:
134 Renfrew Street
Glasgow G3 6ST
Tel: 0141 332 7716

Edinburgh:
131 East Claremont Street
Edinburgh EH7 4JA
Tel: 0131 558 3888

www.mandors.co.uk

ULTIMATE CRAFT
149 Stoke Newington High Street
London N16 0NY
Tel: 020 7923 7923

V V ROULEAUX
102 Marylebone Lane
London W1U 2QD
Tel: 0207 224 5179
www.vvrouleaux.com

USA

B AND J FABRICS
525 7th Avenue (corner of 38th street)
New York, NY, 10018
Tel: 212-354-8150
www.bandjfabrics.com

BOLT
2136 NE Alberta St
Portland, Oregon 97211
Tel: 503.287.2658
www.boltfabricboutique.com

THE COMMON THREAD
701 S Lamar Suite E
Austin, Texas 78704
Tel: 512-445-7270
www.commonthreadfabric.com

FABRIC DEPOT
700 SE 122ND Avenue
Portland, Oregon 97233
Tel: 503-252-9530
www.fabricdepot.com

M&J TRIMMING
1008 Sixth Avenue
(Between 37th & 38th St)
New York, NY 10018
Tel: 1-800-9-MJTRIM
www.mjtrim.com

PURL SOHO
459 Broome Street
New York, NY 10013
Tel: (212) 420-8796
www.purlsoho.com

AUSTRALIA & NZ

BUTTON BAR
Shop 13
Ground Floor
Adelaide Arcade
Adelaide 5000
South Australia
Tel: 08 8223 1610
www.adelaidearcade.com.au/
buttonbar.php

THE FABRIC STORE
Brisbane:
38 Wandoo Street
Fortitude Valley, QLD 4006
Tel: 617 3852 55 80

Melbourne:
184 Brunswick Street
Fitzroy, Melbourne 3065
Tel: 613 9416 4455

Sydney:
21 Cooper Street
Surry Hills, NSW, 2010
Tel: 02 92112217

Auckland:
139 Newton Road
Newton, Auckland 1010
Tel: (09) 366 1991

www.thefabricstore.com.au/
www..globalfabrics.co.nz

L'UCCELLO
Room 205, Level 2
37 Swanston Street
Melbourne VIC 3000
Tel: 9639 0088
www.luccello.com.au

MORRIS & SONS
50 York Street
Sydney NSW 2000
029299 8588
Level 1, 234 Collins Street
Melbourne VIC 3000
Tel: 039654 0888
www.morrisandsons.com.au

TESSUTI FABRICS
Sydney:
110 Commonwealth St.
Surry Hills, NSW, 2010
Tel: 02 9211 5536

20/369 Victoria Ave
Chatswood, NSW, 2067
Tel: 02 9415 3357

Melbourne:
141 Flinders Lane, VIC, 3000
Tel: 03 9654 4566

www.tessuti.com.au

KATIE ALLEN

After an agonising decision on whether to work in a costume shop or study journalism, life-long crafter Katie Allen went for the latter and has spent most of the last seven years writing, editing or working on websites. Along the way she published her own DIY feminist magazine *Fat Quarter*, worked at *Knitting Magazine* and is now the web editor of *www.thebookseller.com* and *www.welovethisbook.com*. Katie never lost the love of making things and has managed to combine the two, regularly contributing to crafty publications such as *Mollie Makes*. She still fits in stitching, knitting, cutting and gluing, and spends far too much money on 'necessary' buttons and yarn.

THANK YOU VERY MUCH

To Karen, sewing queen and wonderful mum

Thank you first of all to Kate Pollard at Hardie Grant UK, without whose enthusiasm this book would never have happened. Also thanks to Leonie Morse for her beautiful photography, Jo Byrne for her fabulous designs, and to Caroline Brown for introducing me to Kate – and for publicising *Just Sew Stories*.

Thank you to the team at *The Bookseller* and *We Love This Book*, who have put up with my endless projects with support and good humour.

Hugs and kisses to my friends who have tolerated my disappearance over the months it took to write this book – particularly Bethan, my Ladyfest compatriot Elizabeth, as well as Jen and Steph – and of course to Indie.

Many, many thanks to my family for always being there for me: particularly my lovely Mum, Dad, brother James, Nanny, Grandma, Renato, Pauline and cats Molly, Bertie and Alfie (not that the last three did anything useful).

Lastly, thank you to the Shoreditch Sisters and all the amazing crafty women I have met or who have inspired me. Keep stitching!

Just Sew Stories by Katie Allen

First published in 2012 by Hardie Grant Books

Hardie Grant Books London
Dudley House, North Suite
34–35 Southampton Street
London WC2E 7HF
www.hardiegrant.co.uk

Hardie Grant Books (Australia)
Ground Floor, Building 1
658 Church Street
Melbourne, VIC 3121
www.hardiegrant.com.au

British Library Cataloguing-in-Publication Data. A catalogue record
for this book is available from the British Library.

ISBN 978-1-74270-418-0

Commissioning Editor: Kate Pollard
Cover and internal design: Joanna Byrne
Photography and retouching: Leonie Morse
Colour reproduction: P2 Digital

Printed and bound China by 1010 Printing International Limited

10 9 8 7 6 5 4 3 2 1

JUNE 2013